ECDL® Advanced 2.0

European Computer Driving Licence

Module AM5 - Database

Using Microsoft® Access 2010

This training, which has been approved by ECDL Foundation, includes exercise items intended to assist Candidates in their training for an ECDL Certification Programme. These exercises are not ECDL Foundation certification tests. For information about authorised Test Centres in different national territories, please refer to the ECDL Foundation website at www.ecdl.org

Release ECDL2

D1627684

Published by:

CiA Training Ltd
Business & Innovation Centre
Sunderland Enterprise Park
Sunderland
SR5 2TA
United Kingdom

Tel: +44 (0) 191 549 5002
Fax: +44 (0) 191 549 9005

E-mail: info@ciatraining.co.uk
Web: www.ciatraining.co.uk

ISBN: 978-1-86005-851-6

Important Note

This guide was written for *Microsoft Office 2010* running on *Windows 7*. If using earlier versions of *Windows* some dialog boxes may look and function slightly differently to that described.

A screen resolution of *1024x768* is assumed. Working at a different resolution (or with an application window which is not maximised) may change the look of the dynamic *Office 2010 Ribbon*, which changes to fit the space available.

For example, the **Editing Group** on a full *Ribbon* will contain several buttons, but if space is restricted it may be replaced by an **Editing Button** (which, when clicked, will display the full **Editing Group**).

First published 2010

European Computer Driving Licence, ECDL, International Computer Driving Licence, ICDL, e-Citizen and related logos are all registered Trade Marks of The European Computer Driving Licence Foundation Limited ("ECDL Foundation").

CiA Training Ltd is an entity independent of ECDL Foundation and is not associated with ECDL Foundation in any manner. This courseware may be used to assist candidates to prepare for the ECDL Foundation Certification Programme as titled on the courseware. Neither ECDL Foundation nor **CiA Training Ltd** warrants that the use of this courseware publication will ensure passing of the tests for that ECDL Foundation Certification Programme. This courseware publication has been independently reviewed and approved by ECDL Foundation as covering the learning objectives for the ECDL Foundation Certification Programme.

Confirmation of this approval can be obtained by viewing the relevant ECDL Foundation Certification Programme training material page of the website www.ecdl.org.

The material contained in this courseware publication has not been reviewed for technical accuracy and does not guarantee that candidates will pass the test for the ECDL Foundation Certification Programme. Any and all assessment items and/or performance-based exercises contained in this courseware relate solely to this publication and do not constitute or imply certification by ECDL Foundation in respect of the ECDL Foundation Certification Programme or any other ECDL Foundation test. Irrespective of how the material contained in this courseware is deployed, for •example in a learning management system (LMS) or a customised interface, nothing should suggest to the candidate that this material constitutes certification or can lead to certification through any other process than official ECDL Foundation certification testing.

For details on sitting a test for an ECDL Foundation certification programme, please contact your country's designated National Licensee or visit the ECDL Foundation's website at www.ecdl.org.

Candidates using this courseware must be registered with the National Operator before undertaking a test for an ECDL Foundation Certification Programme. Without a valid registration, the test(s) cannot be undertaken and no certificate, nor any other form of recognition, can be given to a candidate. Registration should be undertaken with your country's designated National Licensee at an Approved Test Centre.

Downloading the Data Files

The data files associated with these exercises must be downloaded from our website. Go to *www.ciatraining.co.uk/data* and follow the on screen instructions to download the appropriate data files.

By default, the data files will be installed to **CIA DATA FILES \ Advanced ECDL \ AM5 Access 2010 Data** in your **Documents** library\folder (or **My Documents** in *Windows XP*).

If you prefer, the data can be supplied on CD at an additional cost. Contact the Sales team at *info@ciatraining.co.uk*.

Aims

To demonstrate the ability to use a database application on a personal computer.

To understand and accomplish more advanced operations associated with database design.

To demonstrate some of the more advanced features including field properties, relationships, joins, action queries and macros.

Objectives

After completing the guide the user will be able to:

- Create databases
- Design tables and set field properties
- Perform advanced queries
- Create and amend relationships
- Change field properties
- Create forms and form controls
- Create reports and grouped reports
- Import and export data
- Create action queries
- Create and run macros.

Assessment of Knowledge

At the end of this guide is a section called the **Record of Achievement Matrix**. Before the guide is started it is recommended that the user completes the matrix to measure the level of current knowledge.

Tick boxes are provided for each feature. **1** is for no knowledge, **2** some knowledge and **3** is for competent.

After working through a section, complete the matrix for that section and only when competent in all areas move on to the next section.

Contents

Section 1
Fundamentals

By the end of this Section you should be able to:

Understand Database Concepts

Understand SQL

Create a Database

Design a Table

To gain an understanding of the above features, work through the **Driving Lessons** in this **Section**.

For each **Driving Lesson**, read the **Park and Read** instructions, without touching the keyboard, then work through the numbered steps of the **Manoeuvres** on the computer. Complete the **Revision Exercise(s)** at the end of the section to test your knowledge.

Driving Lesson 1 - Database Concepts

▣ Park and Read

Applications for Databases

Databases are used to maintain and retrieve data in various ways; they can certainly help to make an organisation more streamlined and efficient. Many companies use database driven **dynamic websites**; this allows them to update prices and product information, maintain online mailing lists and lets their customers search the data, for example. **Website content management systems** allow non-technical users to make changes and are used as a maintenance tool to create and manage web content. Databases can also be designed to be used as **customer relationship management systems**. Information is stored on current and prospective customers; it can be used to improve services to customers by targeted sales and marketing. **Enterprise resource planning databases** contain data for various business functions in an integrated form. For example, they can be used to control manufacturing, logistics, distribution, inventories, shipping and invoicing.

Database Models

The specification describing how a database is structured and used is known as a **database model**. The main models are:

hierarchical - one of the first models to be widely accepted and used. Records contain groups of parent/child relationships, similar to a tree structure. This model is fast and simple to use, but inflexible because it only contains one-to-many relationships.

relational - data is organised logically in a set of related tables. It can be accessed or reassembled in many different ways without having to reorganise the database tables. A relational database is relatively easy to create and access and is easy to add to.

object-oriented - data is represented by objects. These models do not all support SQL (see DL 3) and so have their limitations.

⌒ Manoeuvres

1. If you have an active internet connection, start your browser application and view the web site **www.ciatraining.co.uk**.

2. Use the links to search for information on any product, **ECDL Advanced** for example. All the information that is presented (icons, description, content, etc.) is held on a dynamic database. As we release new materials, the database is updated and the information is automatically available immediately to users of our web site.

3. Close the site and your browser.

Driving Lesson 2 - Database Development

▣ Park and Read

There are various stages in the "life cycle" of a database.

Logical Design

The first and most important stage is the design, which has to be logical and take into account everything that the database is to be used for; possible future development should also be considered. One way to design a database system is to define the output that is required from the system, then design the various components to achieve that result.

Database Creation

Next is the database creation - the setting up of tables, relationships, forms for data input, query and report definitions. This requires good technical knowledge of a database application.

Data Entry

Once the basic structure has been created, the starting data must be input. This can be a very long process if it has to be done manually, but there are options to import data from other applications.

Data Maintenance

Once the database is running it must be managed. A database is only useful if the integrity of the data is maintained. New information must be added and obsolete data removed promptly. In a large database, a database administrator may be required to do this task.

Information Retrieval

The database can then be interrogated and information retrieved via queries, forms and reports. Sometimes users are restricted to using only the components that are provided, sometimes they will be allowed to build their own queries, reports, etc.

In a large organisation there may be different people for each of the stages above. In a small organisation, one person may have to do it all.

Driving Lesson 3 - SQL

Park and Read

When a query is created in *Access*, the application converts this into a program in a language called **SQL, Structured Query Language**. This language is very widely used across many computing platforms and can be used to write systems in its own right. There is no need for the average user to ever deal with the SQL code behind queries, but it is useful to know about it.

Manoeuvres

1.   Start *Access* and open the **Supermarket** database.

*Any **Security Warning** banner can be ignored throughout this guide unless specifically instructed.*

2.   Locate the **Foodstuff** query from the **Navigation pane**.

3.   Double click **Foodstuff** to run the query.

4.   Click the drop down arrow on the **View** button and select **Design View** to see the design criteria. The query selects records with a **Category** of **Foodstuffs** from the **Stock** table and displays the fields **Product Ref.**, **Item** and **Category**.

5.   Click the drop down arrow on the **View** button and select **SQL View** to see the design criteria. The **SQL** code for the query is displayed.

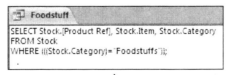

6.   Click the **Close** button, [×], to close the **SQL** view.

7.   Close the database.

Driving Lesson 4 - Creating a Database

▣ Park and Read

The following Driving Lessons demonstrate how to create a database from scratch. In this example, an **Antiquities** database will record sales of ancient artefacts.

↱ Manoeuvres

1. On the *Access* opening screen, make sure the **Blank database** option is selected. A **Blank database** panel is shown on the right of the screen.

2. Use the ☐ button to browse for a location to put your database. Locate the data folder containing the supplied data for this guide.

ⅈ   *The data files for the exercises in this guide are supplied in Access 2007 format (with .accdb extension). Make sure all prompts for file type reflect this.*

3. In the **File name** box, type **Antiquities** and click ⸢ OK ⸤, then on the **Blank database** panel, click the **Create** button.

4. The new **Database Window** is now visible with the database name in the **Title Bar** at the top.

5. Leave the database open.

Driving Lesson 5 - Creating Tables

▣ Park and Read

Tables can be created using a wizard. A wizard gives step by step instructions for the initial setting up and applies default formatting, such as date formats and number formats. Alternatively a table can be created in **Design View** which allows a free hand for formatting.

↰ Manoeuvres

1. The new database shows a default new table (Table1) in **Datasheet** view, with one field named **ID**. This could be used as the first table in the database, but this exercise will demonstrate a more general method of adding new tables. First close the default table, **Table1** by right clicking on the **Table1** tab ⊞ Table1 , and selecting **Close** from the shortcut menu.

> ⓘ *The databases supplied for this guide all use the default **Tabbed Document** format, i.e. all open objects are displayed in the same window with tabs along the top to select them. The functions of **Close, Save** and **View** for any object are easily available by right clicking the tab.*

> ⓘ *The exercises will still work if you use the alternative **Overlapping Windows** format but some of the screen shots will look different. To change the format, click the **File** tab and select **Options**. The format is set on the **Current Database** page, under **Document Window Options**.*

2. Display the **Create** tab and click the **Table Design** button. A new blank table will be opened in **Design View**. This table will not be named until it is saved.

3. In the first row, type **Artefact** in the **Field Name** column.

4. Press <Tab> to move to the next column. **Text** appears in the **Data Type** column. Press <Tab>.

5. The cursor is now in the **Description** column; this column is optional. Enter **Type of Artefact** into this column, then press <Tab>.

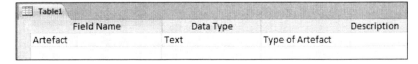

Field Name	Data Type	Description
Artefact	Text	Type of Artefact

6. For the next **Field Name**, enter **Date Sold** and press <Tab>.

continued over

Driving Lesson 5 - Continued

7. Click on the drop down list in the **Data Type** field and select **Date/Time** from the selection.

8. Press **<Tab>** to move into the **Description** column and type **Date the artefact was sold** then press **<Tab>** again.

9. Enter **Price** as the third field name, **<Tab>**, then select **Currency** as the **Data Type** and enter **Selling price** as the description.

10. The next **Field Name** is **Quantity Sold**, the **Data Type** is **Number** and the **Description** is **Number of artefacts sold**.

11. For the next field enter **Information**, the **Data Type** is **Memo** and the **Description** is **History and identifying features**.

i *Memo is used when the field is likely to contain more than 255 characters, which is the maximum allowed by* **Text***.*

12. For the final field, enter the name **Web Address**, a **Data Type** of **Hyperlink** and a **Description** of **Related web site?**

13. Display the **Home** tab and switch to **Datasheet View** by clicking the **View** button. You will be prompted to save the table.

14. Click **Yes. The Save As** dialog box appears.

15. Enter **Artefact Sales** as the table name and click **OK**.

16. There will be a prompt to create a primary key for the table. Click **No** to save the table without creating a primary key. Primary keys are covered in a later exercise.

17. Close the table and the database.

Driving Lesson 6 - Revision

This is not an ECDL test. Testing may only be carried out through certified ECDL test centres. This covers the features introduced in this section and in lower level guides. Try not to refer to the preceding Driving Lessons while completing it.

1. Create a new database named **Stock** and create a table containing the following fields in **Design View**:

Field Name	Data Type	Field Size/Format
Ref	Number	Long Integer
Item	Text	30
Bought by	Text	30
Supplier	Text	2
Price	Currency	
Last Ordered	Date/Time	Short Date
Stock	Number	Long Integer

2. Save the table as **Stationery**, without defining a **Primary Key**.

3. Close the table, saving the design.

4. Close the database.

5. Open the database **Order System**.

6. Click the **Relationships** button on the **Database Tools** tab, or the **Table Tools – Design** tab, to see how the four tables are related. Close the **Relationships** window.

7. Open the query **Example1** in **Design View**. The data in this query comes from how many different tables?

8. Run the query. The data is presented in a single list, regardless of the fact that it is from different tables. Close the query and the database.

*Answers are shown in the **Answers** section at the end of this guide.*

If you experienced any difficulty completing the Revision, refer back to the Driving Lessons in this section. Then redo the Revision.

Once you are confident with the features, complete the Record of Achievement Matrix referring to the section at the end of the guide. Only when competent move on to the next Section.

Section 2
Field Properties

By the end of this Section you should be able to:

Create Lookup Fields

Set and Modify Default Values

Set Mandatory Fields

Create Validation Rules and Text

Create Input Masks

To gain an understanding of the above features, work through the **Driving Lessons** in this **Section**.

For each **Driving Lesson**, read the **Park and Read** instructions, without touching the keyboard, then work through the numbered steps of the **Manoeuvres** on the computer. Complete the **Revision Exercise(s)** at the end of the section to test your knowledge.

Driving Lesson 7 - Lookup Fields

⊞ Park and Read

When creating a table, a field can be defined that that already contains all the possible values that can be entered. This is called a **Lookup Field** and will speed up data input and reduce typing mistakes, because at data entry time there is no need to enter any values, merely select an entry from the presented list. The field can be set so that only entries from the list will be accepted.

There are two options: either the possible values for the field will be manually typed into the field definition, or the field will lookup its possible values from another table in the database. The first option is covered in this lesson, and is used when there are not many values to choose from and they are not expected to change very often.

⌒ Manoeuvres

1. Open the **Custom Computers** database. Open the **Repairs** table in **Design View**. A new lookup field is to be created, called **Processed By**.

2. Position the cursor under **Date** in the **Field Name** column. Enter the **Field Name** as **Processed by** and from **Data Type** choose **Lookup Wizard**. After a few seconds the **Lookup Wizard** appears.

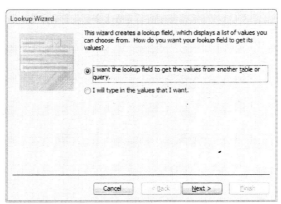

3. From the **Lookup Wizard** choose **I will type in the values that I want** and click **Next**.

4. Specify the **Number of columns:** as **1** and enter the following values into **Col 1**, separating each entry using the <Tab> key: **Davison**, **Jones**, **Hussan** and **Peters**.

5. Click **Next**. The label **Processed by** is correct. Click **Finish** to create the **Lookup Field**.

continued over

Driving Lesson 7 - Continued

6. Save the table and switch to **Datasheet View**. The new field is displayed.

7. **Davison** processed **Job No 1**. Click in **Processed by** for **Job No 1**, click on the down arrow and choose **Davison** from the list.

8. Click in **Processed By** for **Job No 2** and enter the single character **H**. **Hussan** appears in **Processed By** for **Job No 2**. Press the <**Enter**> key.

9. Switch to **Design View**. In **Field Properties**, select the **Lookup** tab.

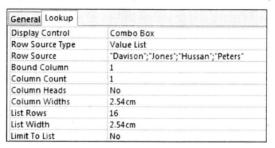

General	Lookup
Display Control	Combo Box
Row Source Type	Value List
Row Source	"Davison";"Jones";"Hussan";"Peters"
Bound Column	1
Column Count	1
Column Heads	No
Column Widths	2.54 cm
List Rows	16
List Width	2.54 cm
Limit To List	No

10. Row Source shows the entries that appear in the field and these can be amended here. Peters leaves the company and is replaced by Cowell. Highlight the text Peters and type Cowell.

11. Change the **Limit To List** option to **Yes**. Save the changes to the table and then switch back to **Datasheet View**.

12. Try to enter the name **Chapman** in the **Processed By** field of one of the records. A message will appear.

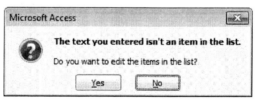

Microsoft Access

The text you entered isn't an item in the list.

Do you want to edit the items in the list?

[Yes]   [No]

13. Because **Limit To List** is set, only the names in the **Lookup** field list box will be accepted. Click **No** and then select **Cowell** from the list.

ℹ *The **Yes** option will allow the list to be edited directly without switching to **Design View**.*

14. Switch to **Design View**, click in the **Processed By** field and select the **Lookup** tab in **Field Properties**.

15. Click the drop down arrow in the **Display Control** field and select **Text Box**. The field is no longer a lookup field.

16. Save the table and leave it open for the next Driving Lesson.

Driving Lesson 8 - Lookup a Table

▣ Park and Read

It is also possible for a **Lookup Field** to look up values from a different table in the database. This can be useful to maintain integrity between tables. For example, a table of customer orders may contain a customer field. If this is made a lookup field to the **Customer** table, orders can only be entered for customer already on the **Customer** table.

Manoeuvres

1. Display the **Repairs** table in **Design View**. The **Engineer** field is to be changed to a **Lookup** field.

2. Click in the **Engineer** field and from **Data Type** choose **Lookup Wizard**.

3. This time choose the option **I want the lookup field to get the values from another table or query.** Click **Next**.

4. Select the **Engineers** table and click **Next**.

5. Select **Engineer Name** from the left and click ⟦ > ⟧ to select it. Click **Next**.

6. Sorting is not required. Click **Next**.

7. The column width should be acceptable, click **Next**.

8. The label **Engineer** is correct. Click **Finish** to create the **Lookup Field**. You will be prompted to save the table. Click **Yes**.

9. Switch to **Datasheet View**, click in any **Engineer** field and click the drop down arrow. Only names from the **Engineers** table will be available.

10. Close the table and the database.

Driving Lesson 9 - Default Values

▣ Park and Read

A **Default Value** is a value that is automatically entered into a particular field of every new record. When records are added, the default value can either be accepted or changed.

The default value is entered in the **Field Properties** area when in **Design View**, in the **Default Value** box.

⌒ Manoeuvres

1. In the **CiA** database, open the **Order Details** table in **Design View**.

2. Select the **Amount** field and position the cursor in the **Default Value** field property.

3. Enter **1**. Every new record will now automatically appear with the number 1 already inserted in the field. This value can be overwritten if required.

4. Save the table and switch to **Datasheet View**. Add a new record with the following details:

Order Ref	Product Ref	Line Number	Amount
225	TA1	1	

5. **1** should automatically be in the **Amount** field. This is the correct figure for this record so close the table.

6. Open the **Orders** table in **Design View**.

7. Select the **Order Date** field and in the **Default Value** enter **=Date()**. This will automatically show the current date for the next new record.

8. Set the **Paid** field **Default Value** to **No**. Save the changes and switch to **Datasheet View** and view the new record row at the bottom of the table.

9. Notice how today's date is in **Order Date** and **Paid** shows **No**. Remember, the default values can be changed when entering records.

10. Close the table then open the **Order Details** table in **Design View**.

11. Change the default value for **Amount** to **2**, save the table and switch to **Datasheet View**.

12. View the new record row and notice how **Amount** shows the modified default value.

13. Close the table but leave the database open.

Driving Lesson 10 - Setting a Mandatory Field

▣ Park and Read

Some fields in a database will be essential to maintain the usefulness of the system. For these fields, it is possible to set field properties so that the field is mandatory or required, i.e. it <u>must</u> always be completed.

It will then be impossible to add a new record to the table without data in this field.

↱ Manoeuvres

1.   Using the **CiA** database, open the **Customer Details** table in **Design View**.

2.   To ensure rapid contact with all customers, the **Telephone** number is to be made a mandatory field. Select the **Field Name** for **Telephone**.

3.   Click at the far right of the **Required** field property. The default value for this property is **No**. This means that a record can be added to the table without an entry in this field.

4.   Select **Yes** from the drop down list. Now any record added to the table <u>must</u> have an entry in this field, or the addition will not be accepted.

5.   Save the table. As a new rule has been defined, any existing data in the table may not now be valid. The following message will appear:

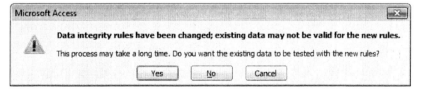

6.   There are three options. Yes will test the existing data with the new rule. No will not test the existing data but will apply the validation to all new records. Cancel will return to the Design View. Select Yes.

7.   Testing will start and because there is an existing record on the table which does not match the rule, i.e. without a telephone number, a dialog box will appear giving three options.

continued over

Driving Lesson 10 - Continued

8. Read the options, then click **Yes** to retain the new settings and continue the testing.

9. Switch to **Datasheet View**.

10. Enter a telephone number for **Customer Ref 30**.

11. Start a new record and enter the following details:

    (32), Mr Vikram Singh, Exotic Foods, High Street, Newcastle, NE1 2JG.

12. Press **<Tab>** to leave the **Telephone** field blank.

13. Tab to the end of the record. The following warning appears:

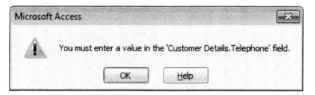

14. Click **OK** and enter the following telephone number: **0191 2661111**.

15. Leave the table open.

Driving Lesson 11 - Validation Rules/Text

▣ Park and Read

Validation Rules are used to set the requirements of the text that the user enters into a particular field. It defines the only permitted entries that the user may make.

If text which breaks the validation rule is entered, a message displaying some pre-set **Validation Text** will be displayed, as defined by the user.

Validation rules and text are defined in the **Field Properties** when viewing a table in **Design View**.

⌒ Manoeuvres

1. View the **Customer Details** table in **Design View**.

2. Select the **Title** field and position the cursor in the **Validation Rule** field property. Enter the following text.

   Mr or Mrs or Miss or Ms or Dr

ℹ️ *This defines the permitted entries for this field. Only these 5 titles will be allowed.*

3. In the **Validation Text** property, enter

   The title must be one of the following: Mr, Mrs, Miss, Ms or Dr.

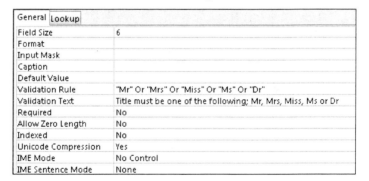

General Lookup	
Field Size	6
Format	
Input Mask	
Caption	
Default Value	
Validation Rule	"Mr" Or "Mrs" Or "Miss" Or "Ms" Or "Dr"
Validation Text	Title must be one of the following; Mr, Mrs, Miss, Ms or Dr
Required	No
Allow Zero Length	No
Indexed	No
Unicode Compression	Yes
IME Mode	No Control
IME Sentence Mode	None

ℹ️ *This defines the message that will appear if any text is entered that does not match the list defined in the **Validation Rule**.*

4. Save the table. Because the rules for the data have changed, the option for testing the existing data will be displayed.

continued over

Driving Lesson 11 - Continued

5. Click **Yes** at the prompt to test the data. There should be no exceptions found.

6. Check in **Datasheet View** and confirm that all the existing data already fits the new validation rule.

7. Start a new record. In the **Title** field enter **Sir**. Press <Tab>. The following message appears:

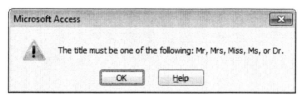

8. This is because **Sir** does not match any of the entries in the **Validation Rule**. Click **OK**.

9. Enter **Mr** in the **Title** field. Press <Tab>. As **Mr** is one of the values included in the **Validation Rule** it allows this to be entered.

10. Fill in the rest of the record with your own details, changing the **Title** to one of the other allowed values if necessary.

11. To edit the validation rule, switch to **Design View**.

12. Select the **Title** field and click at the end of the **Validation Rule** field property, after **"Dr"**.

13. Type in **Or "Sir"**.

14. Amend the **Validation Text** property to include **Sir**.

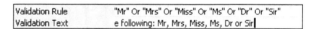

| Validation Rule | "Mr" Or "Mrs" Or "Miss" Or "Ms" Or "Dr" Or "Sir" |
| Validation Text | e following: Mr, Mrs, Miss, Ms, Dr or Sir |

15. Save the table, select **Yes** at the prompt and switch to **Datasheet View**.

16. Start a new record and type **Sir** in the **Title** field. Press <Tab>. As the validation rule has been edited, **Sir** is now a permitted entry and does not result in an error message.

17. Click the **Undo** button, on the **Quick Access Toolbar** to cancel this record entry.

18. Leave the table open for the next Driving Lesson.

Driving Lesson 12 - Input Masks

▣ Park and Read

Input Masks control how data is entered and displayed in a field. The **Input Mask** field property in **Design View** is used. A combination of different symbols is entered, which defines the way in which data in that field is expected to be entered, and how it will be shown. The symbols used are:

Mask Character	Used for
0	Number - entry required.
9	Number - entry not required.
#	Number, + or -, or space - entry not required.
L	Letter - entry required.
?	Letter - entry not required.
A	Letter or Number - entry required.
a	Letter or Number - entry not required.
&	Any character or space - entry required.
C	Any character or space - entry not required.
. ,	Decimal point and thousands separators.
: /	Date and time separators.
<	Converts characters to the right to lowercase.
>	Converts characters to the right to uppercase.
!	Mask fills from right to left.
\	Makes the character that follows to be displayed as itself, e.g. \9 will be displayed as 9.

A **Wizard** is available with some preset masks.

⟳ Manoeuvres

1. Display the **Customer Details** table in **Design View**.

2. Select the **Telephone** field and click in the **Input Mask** field property.

3. The **Build** button appears [...]. Click on it once to view the **Input Mask Wizard**.

4. Select **Phone Number** from the **Input Mask** box.

continued over

Driving Lesson 12 - Continued

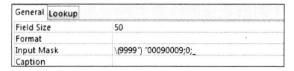

*The predefined masks presented by the **Input Mask Wizard** are region dependent. The picture above shows the masks for UK installations. Different regions will display ·different formats for the same mask (such as Phone Number) and possibly different masks (the US has a Zip Code mask for example). The operation of mask characters and techniques for creating and applying masks are always the same.*

5.   Click **Next**.

6.   Click **Next** on this screen without changing any settings.

7.   Choose to store the data **With the symbols in the mask...** and click **Next**.

8.   Click **Finish**. The mask appears in the **Telephone** field property. The **9** signifies that a number <u>may</u> be entered at that position, the **0** signifies a number <u>must</u> be entered. Both signify a numeric entry only. The mask characters end at the first semicolon.

General	Lookup	
Field Size	50	
Format		
Input Mask	\(9999") "00090009;0;_	
Caption		

9.   Save the table and switch to **Datasheet View**. Notice existing data is not checked against the mask. Add a new record entering any details, but leave the **Telephone** field blank. This results in an error message because the field is now **Required**.

continued over

Driving Lesson 12 - Continued

10. Try to enter **abc** in the **Telephone** field. This will not be allowed, the entry must be numeric.

11. Type **123** and press **<Enter>**. An error message will be shown, including the format of the appropriate input mask.

Microsoft Office Access

ⓘ The value you entered isn't appropriate for the input mask '\(9999") "00090009;0;_' specified for this field.

OK   Help

12. Click **OK**.

13. Highlight the **123** entry and delete it.

14. Position the cursor immediately after the brackets and type **1234567**. The entry should look like (____)**1234567**. This fits the mask and should be accepted.

15. The mask can be modified directly in **Field Properties** without using the Wizard. Switch to **Design View** and change the mask to \(**0009**")"**00090009; 0;_**. The first three zeros means that at least 3 numbers of an area code <u>must</u> be entered.

16. Save the table and switch to **Datasheet View**. Start a new record, entering any details. A telephone number without an area code will not now be accepted. Enter **(0123) 4567890** and press **<Enter>**.

17. Switch to **Design View**. Select the **Telephone** field and click in the **Input Mask** field property.

18. Click and drag to highlight the entire content of the **Input Mask** field and press **<Delete>**. The **Input Mask** is removed.

19. Save the table and close it.

20. Close the database.

Driving Lesson 13 - Revision

This is not an ECDL test. Testing may only be carried out through certified ECDL test centres. This covers the features introduced in this section. Try not to refer to the preceding Driving Lessons while completing it.

1. Open the **Houses** database. Open the **Property** table in **Design View**.

2. Change the **Type of Property** field to be a **Lookup** field with the entries **House, Apartment, Town House**.

3. For the **Glazing** field, create a **Validation Rule** that will only accept the following values: **None, Standard, Double**, and **Tinted**.

4. Create **Validation Text** to go with the **Validation Rule**.

5. Set the **Type of Property** and **Glazing** fields to be **Mandatory**.

6. Save the table and close the database.

7. Open the **Premises** database. Open the **Offers** table in **Design View**.

8. Change the **Property Ref** field in the **Offers** table to be a **Lookup** field that will look up possible values from the **Property Ref** field in the **Commercial** table.

9. Use **Limit To List** to ensure this field only accepts one of these entries.

10. Save the table and display it in **Datasheet View**. Add a new record to test the **Lookup** field.

11. Close the table and database.

If you experienced any difficulty completing the Revision, refer back to the Driving Lessons in this section. Then redo the Revision.

Once you are confident with the features, complete the Record of Achievement Matrix referring to the section at the end of the guide. Only when competent move on to the next Section.

Section 3
Queries

By the end of this Section you should be able to:

Create Sum and Count Queries

Use Group By in Queries

Show Average, Maximum and Minimum Values

Create Calculated Fields

Create Parameter Queries

Use Wildcards

To gain an understanding of the above features, work through the **Driving Lessons** in this **Section**.

For each **Driving Lesson**, read the **Park and Read** instructions, without touching the keyboard, then work through the numbered steps of the **Manoeuvres** on the computer. Complete the **Revision Exercise(s)** at the end of the section to test your knowledge.

Driving Lesson 14 - Sum

Park and Read

Queries can be created in *Access*, where summary values only are displayed rather than individual records. The summary values can be displayed for the whole query, or as subtotals for certain groups of records. Common summary calculations include finding the total and average of a set of figures, the maximum and minimum value and counting the number of records. These calculations are carried out on a **Total** line within the query.

Manoeuvres

1.   Open the **Premises** database which holds information on commercial properties for sale in a large city. Create a new query in **Design View** based on the **Commercial** table. Place the **Location** and **Price** fields on to the query grid.

2.   Make sure the **Design** tab is selected and click on the **Totals** button. A new row appears on the grid marked **Total:** with the default entry of **Group By**.

3.   Click in the **Total** box for the **Price** field, then click on the down arrow to display the drop down list. Select **Sum** from this list.

Field:	Location	Price
Table:	Commercial	Commercial
Total:	Group By	Sum
Sort:		
Show:	✓	✓
Criteria:		
or:		

4.   Run the query.

Location	SumOfPrice
Central Area	£1,237,000.00
DockLand	£525,000.00
Enterprise Centre	£574,000.00
Industrial Park	£387,000.00
Riverside Complex	£907,000.00
Valley Grove	£551,000.00

5.   Note that this is a **Summary Query**, only totals are shown. The records are grouped by **Location**, and the **Price** is totalled for each different location.

6.   Switch back to the **Design View** and leave the query open for the next Driving Lesson.

i *The **Total** row can be removed by clicking* Σ *again.*

Driving Lesson 15 - Count

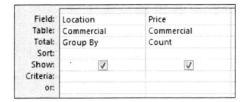 **Park and Read**

The **Count** calculation is another summary calculation, which counts how many entries in a query have a value in a particular field, including duplicate values. It does not count null entries, i.e. empty fields.

Manoeuvres

1. Using the query from the previous Driving Lesson, change the **Total** box for the **Price** field to **Count**.

Field:	Location	Price
Table:	Commercial	Commercial
Total:	Group By	Count
Sort:		
Show:	☑	☑
Criteria:		
or:		

2. Run the query. The answer table now shows a count of how many premises (that have a price) are in each location group.

Location	CountOfPrice
Central Area	8
DockLand	6
Enterprise Centre	5
Industrial Park	5
Riverside Complex	9
Valley Grove	7

 Take care when choosing which field to use in the count. If any records on the table above did not have an entry in the price field, they would not be included in the count.

3. Switch back to the **Design View**.

4. Select the **Location** column and delete it.

5. Run the query. All records (that have a price) are counted and a single value is displayed.

6. Switch back to the **Design View** and delete the **Price** column.

7. Leave the empty query open for the next Driving Lesson.

Driving Lesson 16 - Average Values

▣ Park and Read

Avg is another summary calculation. It calculates the average of all values in a field. It is selected from the **Total** row in the query grid, in a similar way as **Count** and **Sum**. All summary calculations can be combined with selection criteria to obtain statistics on certain parts of the data.

Manoeuvres

1. Using the query from the previous Driving Lesson, add the field **Type of Premises**. Leave the **Total** box as **Group By**.

2. Add the field **Price** to the grid. Select the calculation **Avg** in the **Total** box.

3. Run the query. The average price for each type of premises is shown.

Type of Premises ▾	AvgOfPrice ▾
Conference Unit	£90,000.00
Exhibition Hall	£209,333.33
Manufacturing Unit	£90,444.44
Office Premises	£116,352.94
Store Unit	£57,285.71

4. Switch back to Design View. Include the Lift field on the grid, leave its Total value as Group by and enter Yes in its criteria.

Field:	Type of Premises	Price	Lift
Table:	Commercial	Commercial	Commercial
Total:	Group By	Avg	Group By
Sort:			
Show:	✓	✓	✓
Criteria:			Yes
or:			

5. Run the query again to see the average property prices by type of premises, but this time only for properties with a lift.

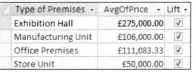

Type of Premises ▾	AvgOfPrice ▾	Lift ▾
Exhibition Hall	£275,000.00	✓
Manufacturing Unit	£106,000.00	✓
Office Premises	£111,083.33	✓
Store Unit	£50,000.00	✓

6. Switch back to **Design View**. Remove the **Lift** column and add a criteria of **store unit** to the **Type of Premises** column.

7. Run the query to see the average price for **Store Units** only.

8. Switch to the **Design View** and delete the **Type of Premises** column.

9. Run the query to see the average **Price** for all premises.

10. Switch to the **Design View** and clear all information from the query grid.

11. Leave the query grid on screen for the next Driving Lesson.

ℹ *Answers are shown in the **Answers** section at the end of this guide.*

Driving Lesson 17 - Maximum and Minimum Values

▣ Park and Read

Max and **Min** are summary calculations showing the maximum and minimum values of specified fields for all selected records. A range of the highest and lowest values in a table can be displayed using the **TopValues** property.

↷ Manoeuvres

1. Using the query from the previous Driving Lesson, place the fields **Location** and **Price** on to the query grid. Add the **Price** field again as a third column.

2. Change the **Total** box for the first **Price** column to **Max** and the second one to **Min**.

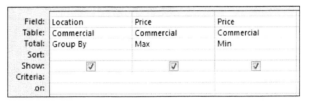

3. Run the query. The results table should contain the maximum and minimum prices in each location.

4. Switch to **Design View** and click the **Totals** button, to remove the **Total** row from the grid. Remove one of the **Price** columns and add the **Address** field to the grid.

5. Define an **Ascending Sort** for the **Price** field.

6. Select **5** in the **Top Values** drop down box, [≡ Return: 5 ▾], in the **Query Setup** group on the **Design** tab.

7. Run the query. Premises with the 5 lowest prices are displayed.

8. Switch to **Design View**, and change the **Price** field sort to **Descending**.

9. Enter **25%** in the **Top Values** drop down box and run the query. The top 25% of records (10 out of 40) in order of **Price** are displayed.

10. Switch to **Design View**, and select **All** in the **Top Values** drop down box.

11. Close the query <u>without</u> saving and close the database.

ⓘ *Answers are shown in the **Answers** section at the end of this guide.*

Driving Lesson 18 - Calculated Fields: Queries

🅿 Park and Read

When a calculation is required in a query, based on the contents of one or more of the available fields, a **Calculated Field** may be used. This is a field that the user creates, to display the results of a calculation defined with an **expression**. The **expression** may involve one or more numerical fields, and involve any mathematical calculations or logical definitions. It allows, for example, two fields to be multiplied together, or for a price field to be multiplied by a percentage, or a discount applied to all values in a particular field.

The name of the new field is entered in the **Field** row of a query grid, followed by a colon, :. The expression is then entered, with field names enclosed in square brackets. Once a calculated field is defined, it can be used like any other field. It can be used for selection, for sorting, or appear in forms and reports.

The standard mathematical symbols are **Add +**, **Subtract -**, **Divide /** and **Multiply ***.

Manoeuvres

1. Open the **Pets** database.

2. Start a new query in **Design View** based on **Pet Details** and place the **Animal**, **Price** and **Number Sold** fields into the grid.

3. In the fourth column enter the following expression in the **Field:** box:

   Total Amount: [Price]*[Number Sold]

4. **Total Amount** is the new field name, **Price** and **Number Sold** are the fields and * is the mathematical operator. This is a new **Calculated Field** that will multiply the price of each animal by the number of each animal sold, and call the answer **Total Amount**.

5. Make sure the **Show** box is checked for the new field.

Field:	Animal	Price	Number Sold	Total Amount: [Price]*[Number Sold]
Table:	Pet Details	Pet Details	Pet Details	
Sort:				
Show:	✓	✓	✓	✓
Criteria:				
or:				

6. Run the query. The answer table will contain the total amount for each type of pet that was sold.

continued over

Driving Lesson 18 - Continued

Query1			
Animal ▾	Price ▾	Number Sold ▾	Total Amount ▾
Rabbit	£30.00	3	£90.00
Fish	£0.80	5	£4.00
Toad	£1.50	6	£9.00
Snake	£13.00	6	£78.00
Dog	£3.50	7	£24.50
Cat	£8.00	9	£72.00
*			0

7.   Once a calculated field has been defined it can be used in the query like any other field. Return to **Design View** and enter **>10** in the criteria for the **Total Amount** field.

8.   Run the query to see only those sales records where the total sales amount is greater than **£10**.

9.   Return to **Design View**. Logical expressions can also be used. Add a new field to the query and add the following expression to the first line:

Size: IIF([Total Amount]>50,"Big","Small")

10.   Run the query. The new field will display **Big** for records with total values greater than £50, and **Small** for all others.

11.   Return to **Design View**. Because the calculated field has not been defined in a table, field properties will not have been specifically set up.

12.   Click in the **Total Amount** column in the query grid to select it. Click **Property Sheet**, 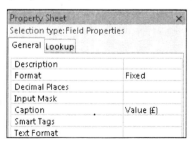 Property Sheet on the **Show/Hide** section of the **Design** tab. The **Property Sheet** is displayed.

13.   Select **Format**, click the drop down arrow and choose **Fixed**.

14.   Select **Caption** and enter the text **Value (£)**. The **Caption** value is only displayed when the query is run, it is not shown on the query grid.

Property Sheet	✕
Selection type: Field Properties	
General Lookup	
Description	
Format	Fixed
Decimal Places	
Input Mask	
Caption	Value (£)
Smart Tags	
Text Format	

15.   Close the **Property Sheet** and run the query to see the changes.

16.   Save the query as **Total Amount** then close the query and the database.

Driving Lesson 19 - Parameter Queries

Park and Read

If a query is being run frequently and all that is changing is the selection criteria for one or two fields, then a **Parameter Query** can be used. A **Parameter Query** displays a dialog box prompting for the criteria information. Once the information is entered, the query is performed, with the entered value being used as the selection criteria. The next time the query is run, a different value can be entered and used, without having to change the query design.

Parameters can be used together with other types of query, such as partial queries using wildcards and range queries.

A query can contain as many parameter values as required. Simply set a parameter value for each required field. Every time the query is run, a dialog box will appear for each field that contains a parameter value. The dialog boxes will appear in the order of the field names on the query grid, from left to right.

Manoeuvres

1.   Open the **Premises** database. Start a new query in **Design View** based on the **Commercial** table and place the following fields on to the grid: **Location, Address, Type of Premises** and **Price**.

2.   To create the parameter query, in the **Location** field enter the following text as the criteria: **[Enter Area Required]**.

Ensure that the prompt text between square brackets is not the same as any field name. For example, [Location] would not work because there is a field with that name, but [Location?] would be OK.

3.   Run the query. A dialog box appears. Notice the text entered in the criteria appears as the prompt text. The value entered in the entry box will be used as the criteria for **Location**.

4.   Enter **Dockland** and click **OK**. The query is run, showing all premises in Dockland.

continued over

Driving Lesson 19 - Continued

Location	Address	Type of Premises	Price
DockLand	1 Wessington Road	Manufacturing Unit	£120,000.00
DockLand	14a The Union Buildings	Manufacturing Unit	£75,000.00
DockLand	Unit 7 Grantham House	Manufacturing Unit	£80,000.00
DockLand	17 The Port Buildings	Store Unit	£38,000.00
DockLand	Suite 15 Grosvenor Estate	Store Unit	£120,000.00
DockLand	4 Grainger Dock	Manufacturing Unit	£92,000.00
*			

5. Switch back to **Design View**.

6. Add a criteria of **[Which Premises Type?]** to the **Type of Premises** column.

7. Run the query again. This time enter **Riverside Complex** in the **Area** prompt and click **OK**. Enter **Office Premises** in the second prompt and click **OK**.

8. Save the query as **Areas** but leave it open.

9. Parameters can be used with range selections. Return to **Design View**. Delete all existing criteria and add a new criteria to the **Price** field.

    >=[from lower value] and <=[to upper value]

10. Run the query. When the first dialog box appears, enter **100000** and click **OK**.

11. The second dialog box will appear. Enter **200000** and click **OK**. The query shows all premises with values between £100,000 and £200,000.

12. Save the query as **Values**.

13. Close the query and the database.

Driving Lesson 20 - Using Wildcards in a Query

▣ Park and Read

The use of basic wildcard characters **?** and ***** is covered in the standard syllabus for this qualification. There are however further characters which can be used, such as **[ ], !, -, #.**

Manoeuvres

1.   Open the **Staff** database,

2.   Create a new query in **Design View** based on the **Test List** table. Place all fields into the query grid.

3.   In the criteria for **First Name**, type **T?m***. Run the query. All names starting **T?m** are listed, where **?** can be any character.

4.   Switch to **Design View** and change the criteria to **T[aeo]m***.

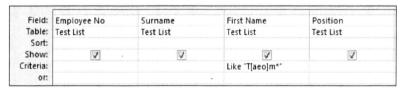

Field:	Employee No	Surname	First Name	Position
Table:	Test List	Test List	Test List	Test List
Sort:				
Show:	✓	✓	✓	✓
Criteria:			Like "T[aeo]m*"	
or:				

ℹ️ *If the criteria is not formatted automatically, the query will not work and you will have to enter **Like "T[aeo]m*"** in full.*

5.   Run the query. Any character from **a**, **e** or **o** is allowed as the wildcard.

6.   Switch to **Design View** and change the criteria to **Like "T[!aeo]m*"**. Run the query. Any character <u>except</u> **a**, **e** or **o** is allowed as the wildcard.

7.   Switch to **Design View** and change the criteria to **Like "T[a-n]m*"**. Run the query. Any character between **a** and **n** is allowed as the wildcard.

8.   Switch to **Design View** and delete the criteria for **First Name**.

9.   In the criteria for **Employee No**, type **Like "5##"**. Run the query. The **#** represents any number. All 3 digit numbers starting with 5 are listed.

10. Switch to **Design View** and change the criteria to **Like "##3"**. Run the query. All 3 digit numbers ending with 3 are listed.

11. Close the query <u>without</u> saving and close the **Staff** database.

Driving Lesson 21 - Revision

This is not an ECDL test. Testing may only be carried out through certified ECDL test centres. This covers the features introduced in this section. Try not to refer to the preceding Driving Lessons while completing it.

1. Open the database **Computer Shop** and create a new query in **Design View** based on the **Repairs** table.

2. Use **Group By** to find the number of engineers.

3. What are the minimum and maximum job prices?

4. What is the total price of all the jobs on the database?

5. Change the query to find the average job price grouped by engineer. Which engineer has the highest average job price?

6. Save the query as **Query21a** and close it.

7. Create a parameter query to ask for a particular engineer then show all the jobs for that engineer above an entered price. Show all fields from the **Repairs** table.

8. Use that query to find how many jobs **Keith** has that cost more than **£100**.

9. Save the query as **Query21b** and close it.

10. Close the database.

11. Open the database **Transport** and create a new query in **Design View** based on the **Buses** table. Include the fields **Fleet Number**, **Size** and **Route**.

12. Use wildcards to select only **Fleet Numbers** that have the following structure: Any 1 character followed by any 1 number followed by the number 5. What is the criteria? How many records are found?

13. Close the query <u>without</u> saving and close the database.

 *Answers are shown in the **Answers** section at the end of this guide.*

If you experienced any difficulty completing the Revision, refer back to the Driving Lessons in this section. Then redo the Revision.

Driving Lesson 22 - Revision

This is not an ECDL test. Testing may only be carried out through certified ECDL test centres. This covers the features introduced in this section. Try not to refer to the preceding Driving Lessons while completing it.

1. Using the **Houses** database and **Property** table, create a new **Summary** query in **Design View**.

2. Use the query to display the total and average **Price** of each property grouped by **Type of Property**.

3. Which type of property has the highest average price?

4. Save the query as **Query22a** and close it.

5. Create a new query on the same table and include the fields **Location, Address, Type of Property, Price** and **Bedrooms**.

6. Create a new calculated field in the query, after the **Bedrooms** field. Name the new field **Rate** and define the calculation as **Price** divided by **Bedrooms**. Format the new field as **Currency**.

7. Display the query in descending order of **Rate**. Which property has the highest value for **Rate**?

8. Change the query so that it prompts for **Location** with the message "**Which Location**".

9. Use the query to find the property in **Rose Mount** with the highest value of **Rate**.

10. Save the query as **Price per Bedroom** and close it and the database.

 *Answers are shown in the **Answers** section at the end of this guide.*

If you experienced any difficulty completing the Revision, refer back to the Driving Lessons in this section. Then redo the Revision.

Once you are confident with the features, complete the Record of Achievement Matrix referring to the section at the end of the guide. Only when competent move on to the next Section.

Section 4
Relationships

By the end of this Section you should be able to:

Apply Primary Keys

Apply and Modify Different Types of Relationship

Query Related Tables

Understand Joins

Apply Referential Integrity

Update and Delete Related Records

Work with Subdatasheets

To gain an understanding of the above features, work through the **Driving Lessons** in this **Section**.

For each **Driving Lesson**, read the **Park and Read** instructions, without touching the keyboard, then work through the numbered steps of the **Manoeuvres** on the computer. Complete the **Revision Exercise(s)** at the end of the section to test your knowledge.

Driving Lesson 23 - Applying a Primary Key

▣ Park and Read

When creating relational databases which use more than one table, it is important to be able to uniquely identify individual records in a table if they are to be referenced from another table. Records are usually identified by specifying a field in the table which contains unique data for each record, e.g. a serial number or identification number. This is then defined as the **Primary Key**.

Use of a **Primary Key** prevents duplication of records in a table and also allows sorting and querying to be performed more efficiently. It also enables the linking of tables.

⌦ Manoeuvres

1. Open the **Custom Computers** database and then the **Computers** table in **Design View**. Make sure the **Design** tab is selected.

2. Click in the **Model** field. Click on the **Primary Key** button in the **Tools** group on the **Design** tab.

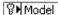 Model

> **i** *The **Primary Key** is applied to the **Model**. field. Notice in the field properties that the **Indexed** property is set to **Yes (No Duplicates)**. This means that there can be no duplicate **Model** in any two records within this table.*

3. This is obviously a bad choice for the **Primary Key** field as it is likely that there will be more than one record in the table for any particular model of computer. Click in the **Serial Number** field and click on the **Primary Key** button again.

4. **Serial Number** is now designated as the **Primary Key** field. This is an ideal choice, as a serial number is a unique identifier for any particular computer.

> **i** *When **Serial Number** was selected as the **Primary Key**, the indicator was automatically removed from the **Model** field.*

5. **Save** and close the table.

6. Open the **Repairs** table in **Design View**. A **Primary Key** is already applied to the **Job No** field.

continued over

Driving Lesson 23 - Continued

7. Notice that the **Repairs** table also contains the computer serial number field, but on this table it is not necessarily unique. There may be several repair jobs for the same computer.

8. A **Primary Key** is just a special index for a table. Click the **Indexes** button on the **Design** tab, to view the **Primary Key** information.

 *The **Index Properties** show that a **Primary Key** field is unique and that **Ignore Nulls** is set to **No**. This means that as well as being unique, a primary key field cannot be left blank in a record.*

9. Close the **Indexes** window and the **Repairs** table.

10. Leave the **Custom Computers** database open.

Driving Lesson 24 - Applying Relationships

🅿 Park and Read

Once tables have been designed and primary keys applied, a **Relationship** may be applied between two or more tables to link them together. Once two or more tables are linked by a relationship, the data from all of the tables may be used to create a single query, form or report.

Relationships are usually applied between tables which contain a common field. Usually, the related field in the first table is the primary key field and is known as the **Primary Table**. In this way, a record in one table can link to further information on another table. The related field in the second table is known as the **Foreign Key**.

Applying relationships allows many smaller tables to be linked together to form the complete database, improving its overall efficiency. In the Driving Lesson below then, if the **Computer** and **Repairs** tables are linked using the common field serial number, there is no need to have all computer details on every repair record. A query on the **Repairs** table will use **Serial Number** to access all related data on the **Computers** table automatically.

This lesson describes the most common type of relationship, **One to Many**. Other types of relationships are introduced over the next few Driving Lessons.

👆 Manoeuvres

1. Display the **Database Tools** tab and click the **Relationships** button. A blank **Relationship** window will be displayed.

2. If the **Show Table** dialog box is not shown, click the **Show Table** button, on the **Relationship Tools Design** tab. This displays the available tables in this database.

continued over

Driving Lesson 24 - Continued

3.   With the **Computers** table highlighted, click to place the table in the **Relationships** window.

4.   Click on the **Repairs** table and again add it to the window then click **Close** to remove the **Show Table** dialog box.

5.   Resize the table boxes to see all of their fields. Notice the **Primary Keys** for each table indicated with a key symbol.

Relationships	
Computers	**Repairs**
⚷ Serial Number	⚷ Job No
Manufacturer	Engineer
Model	Job Description
Year Made	Serial Number
Owner	Date
First Name	Processed by
Title	
Address	
Telephone	
Paid	

6.   Highlight the **Serial Number** field in the **Computers** table.

7.   Drag the **Serial Number** field, from the **Computers** table, over the **Serial Number** field (the foreign key) in the **Repairs** table. Release the mouse when in position.

8.   In the **Edit Relationships** dialog box, note the relationship type is **One-To-Many**. This is the most common type of relationship.

continued over

Driving Lesson 24 - Continued

9. Click <u>Create</u> to create the relationship.

10. Notice how the relationship between the tables is now symbolised by a line, linking the same field, **Serial Number**.

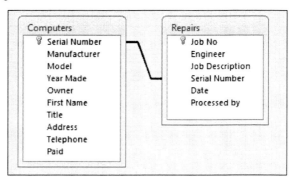

> **i** *The relationship is **One-To-Many**. This means that **one** record from **Computers** can have **many** related records in **Repairs**, i.e. one computer may have had several repairs. The fact that one of the fields in the link is a primary key and the other is not, defines the relationship as **One-To-Many**.*

11. To delete the relationship, right click on the connecting line and select **Delete**. Select **Yes** to confirm the deletion.

> **i** *Any relationship can be modified by right clicking on the connecting line and selecting **Edit Relationship**.*

12. Now click and drag from **Owner** in the **Computers** table to **Engineer** in the **Repairs** table.

13. This is not a valid relationship; the relationship type is shown as **Indeterminate**. Click **Cancel**.

14. Reapply the original relationship between **Serial Number** in both tables and click **Create**.

15. Close the **Relationships** window and select **Yes** when prompted to save the changes to the relationship.

16. Leave the database open for the next Driving Lesson.

Driving Lesson 25 - One-to-One Relationships

▣ Park and Read

A **One-to-One** relationship is used where one record in one table is linked to only one record in another. This can be used to split a large table with many fields, or if part of a table needs to be removed for security reasons, or if the second table contains optional data which is not always required.

Manoeuvres

1. To create a **One-to-One** relationship in the **Custom Computers** database, create a table in **Design View** with two fields, **Job No** and **Charge**.

2. The **Job No** field will have a data type of **Number** and the **Charge** field will be **Currency**.

3. Make the **Job No** field the **Primary Key** and save the table as **Cost**. Close it without adding any data.

4. Open the **Relationships** window showing the existing relationship and use the **Show Table** button to display the dialog box.

5. Select **Cost** then click **Add** to add it to the **Relationships** window. Close the **Show Table** box.

6. Reposition the **Cost** table if necessary, then make the link between **Job No** in the **Repairs** table and **Job No** in the **Cost** table. Because each of these fields is a primary key, this time in the **Edit Relationships** box, the **Relationship Type** is **One-To-One**.

7. Click **Create**.

ℹ️ *As with any relationship, this can be deleted or modified by right clicking on the connecting line and selecting **Delete** or **Edit Relationship**.*

continued over

Driving Lesson 25 - Continued

8. Close the **Relationships** window, saving at the prompt, then open the **Computers** table. Each record has an **expand subdatasheet** button.

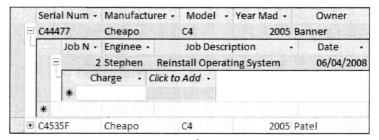

9. Click the expand subdatasheet button next to the first record. The related **Repairs** table is shown – notice that **Serial Number**, the related field in the second table (the foreign key), is not shown.

10. There is also now an expand button in the **Repairs** table. Click on it.

11. The **Cost** table is shown for this record.

12. At the moment there is no data in the **Charge** field. Add a charge of **£50** for this repair.

13. Try adding another charge for this repair. Remember there is a **One-to-One** relationship in force, so only one charge should be allowed. A warning dialog box is displayed as below.

> **Microsoft Access**
>
> The changes you requested to the table were not successful because they would create duplicate values in the index, primary key, or relationship. Change the data in the field or fields that contain duplicate data, remove the index, or redefine the index to permit duplicate entries and try again.
>
> OK   Help

14. Click **OK** once you have read it. To get rid of this useless information click the **Undo** button, or press the <**Esc**> key.

15. The extra entry is deleted and the subdatasheets can be collapsed.

16. Open each subdatasheet in turn and add **Charges** for all **Repairs**.

17. Close the table and the database.

Driving Lesson 26 - Many-to-Many Relationships

▣ Park and Read

A **Many-to-Many** relationship is used when a record in the first table can have many matching records in the second, and vice versa. For example, a single product may have many orders and a single order may be for many products. A single **Many-to-Many** relationship cannot exist. An intermediate **junction table** must be created with **One to Many** links to the two original tables. It must contain two fields: the foreign keys from both tables.

Manoeuvres

1. Open the **CiA** database. To create a **Many-to-Many** relationship between the **Orders** table and the **Products** table it is first necessary to create an intermediate, junction table.

2. Create a new table in **Design View** containing the fields **Order Ref (Number)** and **Product Ref (Text)**.

3. The primary key for this new table will be defined as the combination of both fields (neither individual field will be unique on the table). Click in the area at the left of **Order Ref** to highlight the whole row.

4. Hold down **<Ctrl>** and click at the left of **Product Ref**. Both rows will be highlighted.

5. Click the **Primary Key** button.

Field Name	Data Type
🔑 Order Ref	Number
🔑 Product Ref	Text

6. Save the table as **Junction** and close it.

7. This table would now have to be filled with information about which products were on which orders. To save time such a table has already been created in the database. Open the **Order Details** table in **Datasheet View**, showing the information on each order line.

8. Switch to **Design View**.

Field Name	Data Type	
🔑 Order Ref	Number	Order reference
🔑 Product Ref	Text	Product ordered
Line Number	Number	Order Line
Amount	Number	Quantity ordered

continued over

Driving Lesson 26 - Continued

*In a working database, this table would be maintained as part of the **Order Entry** process.*

9. Close the table and view the **Relationships** window. Place the **Orders**, **Order Details** and **Products** tables on to it.

10. Create a **One-to-Many** relationship between the **Orders** table and the **Order Details** table using the **Order Ref** field.

11. Create a **One-to-Many** relationship between the **Products** table and the **Order Details** table using the **Product Ref** field. The overall effect now is that there is a **Many-to-Many** relationship between the **Orders** and **Products** tables.

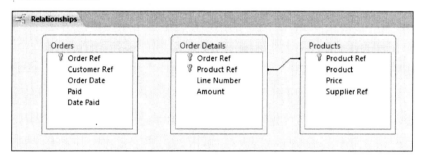

*As with any relationship, these can be deleted or modified by right clicking on the connecting line and selecting **Delete** or **Edit Relationship**.*

12. Close the **Relationships** window, saving when prompted.

13. Create a query based on the three tables shown above.

14. Add **Customer Ref** and **Product** to the grid and specify an **Ascending Sort** on **Customer Ref**.

15. Run the query to see which products have been bought by each customer.

16. Switch to **Design View**, remove the **Customer** sort and specify an **Ascending Sort** on the **Product**.

17. Run the query again to see which customers have bought each product.

18. Close the query <u>without</u> saving and close the database.

Driving Lesson 27 - Applying Joins

▣ Park and Read

Joins describe the links between tables. They affect the way queries select records when related tables are involved.

The default join type, which is applied by *Access* automatically, is an **inner join**. With this type of join, a query will only display records where there is a corresponding entry in <u>both</u> tables. For example, a query on linked **Computers** and **Repairs** tables would only show computers that had a repair. Any computers without a repair job, or jobs without relevant computer records, would <u>not</u> be displayed. This is an important point to remember. Sometimes a linked tables query will not display all the records you expect because of this.

Using the above example, if you wanted to display <u>all</u> computers in a query, whether or not they had a match in the **Repairs** table, you would redefine the link as an **outer join** based on the **Computers** table. An alternative **outer join** based on the **Repairs** table could also be defined, which would show <u>all</u> repair records, even when there was no associated computer record. A **subtract join** is the opposite of an outer join; it includes only those records in one table that <u>don't match</u> any record in the other table.

⌒ Manoeuvres

1. Open the **Custom Computers** database and open the **Computers** table.

2. Create the following record: **B12345A, Bantacom, Pentio, 2007, Smallfoot, Andrew, Mr, 234 Cedar Drive**. Leave all other fields blank.

3. Close the table. The computer is registered but has had no repairs yet.

4. Create a new query in **Design View**. Add the **Computers** table and then the **Repairs** table to the grid. Because there is a relationship defined for these tables the link will be displayed.

continued over

Driving Lesson 27 - Continued

5. Double click the relationship line to display the **Join Properties** dialog box.

6. Notice how join type **1** is selected by default. This is an **inner join**. Click **OK** without making any changes.

7. From **Computers**, place **Serial Number** and **Model** on the grid.

8. From **Repairs**, place **Job No**, **Engineer** and **Date** on the grid.

9. Run the query. Even though the new **Bantacom Pentio** record is in the **Computers** table, it is not shown in the results because <u>only records with repairs</u> are displayed.

10. Switch back to **Design View** and double click the relationship line. To define the link as a **left outer join** based on the **Computers** table, select option **2**.

11. Click **OK** and run the query. The **Pentio** record is now shown, but because it has not been repaired, the last three fields are blank.

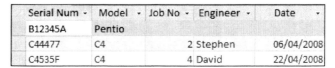

Serial Num ▾	Model ▾	Job No ▾	Engineer ▾	Date ▾
B12345A	Pentio			
C44477	C4		2 Stephen	06/04/2008
C4535F	C4		4 David	22/04/2008

12. Save the query as **Outer join** and close it.

13. Reopen the **Outer join** query in **Design View**. Add the criteria **Is Null** to the **Job No** field.

14. Run the query. Only the **Pentio** record is displayed, because this is the only record <u>without</u> a **Job No**. This is known as a **subtract join** and displays <u>only</u> computers that have <u>no</u> repair.

*The actual link is still an outer join, the **Is Null** criteria makes it a subtract join.*

15. Save the query as **Subtract join** and close it. Close the database.

Driving Lesson 28 - Self Joins

🅿 Park and Read

A **self join** describes the situation where a table needs to be linked to itself. For example, in a **Staff** table, with **Employee Number** as the primary key, there may be a field showing who each employee's manager is, using the manager's employee number. This employee number will already appear as the primary key for a record in the table (managers are also employees). To display the manager's name instead of their number in a query, a link to a copy of the **Staff** table will need to be set up, using **Manager** as the link field.

Manoeuvres

1. Open the **Staff** database and create a new query in **Design View**. At the moment, the manager that each member of staff reports to is only shown in the **Reports To** field as a staff number. A query can be created to display the manager's name, but first a **self join** must be created.

2. To create the self join, add the **Staff List** table to the query grid twice.

ℹ️ *The table itself is not duplicated; it is just referred to by two different names.*

3. The second list is given a different name, **Staff List_1**. To change this, right click on the list and select **Properties** from the shortcut menu.

4. Change the **Alias** entry to **Managers** and close the **Property Sheet**.

5. Drag the **Reports To** field from **Staff List** to the **Employee No** field in the **Managers** to create the link.

6. From **Staff List**, add **Employee No**, **Surname** and **First Name** to the grid and from **Managers**, add **Surname** to the grid again.

continued over

Driving Lesson 28 - Continued

7.   To change the last field title so that it displays **Manager** instead of **Surname**, click anywhere in the last field in the query grid to select it, then click 🖰 Property Sheet from the **Show/Hide** area of the **Design** tab.

8.   Change the **Caption** property to **Manager**.

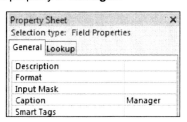

9.   Close the **Property Sheet** and run the query. Widen the columns if required.

Employee No ▾	Staff List.Surname ▾	First Name ▾	Manager ▾
100	Nyder	Peter	Cheshunt
101	Cheshunt	Richard	Singh
112	Myers	Anthony	Singh
301	Lee	Ciara	Myers
321	Chapman	Ian	Cheshunt
403	Morris	Tracy	Cheshunt
500	Valdron	Brian	Myers
505	Kline	William	Cheshunt
509	Jones	Lesley	Cheshunt
536	Singh	Vikram	Singh
688	Chamberlain	Anthony	Cheshunt
704	Parr	Norma	Cheshunt
1000	Ripley	Ellen	Myers

10.   Notice how the manager's name and not their employee number appears in the **Manager** field. This is because the self join created earlier causes the query to look up the corresponding name for each employee number entered in the **Reports To** field and return that value.

ℹ *The actual link in a self join is still either an inner or outer join, it is the fact that it links to a copy of the same table that makes it a self join. Like any relationship, this can be deleted or modified by right clicking on the connecting line and selecting **Delete** or **Edit Relationship**.*

11.   Save the query as **Self join** and close it.

12.   Close the database.

Driving Lesson 29 - Referential Integrity

▣ Park and Read

Referential Integrity is a set of rules which can be applied to relationships, ensuring they are valid and that data is not accidentally deleted or changed. It may be applied when specific conditions are met: the matching field from the primary table is a primary key, the related fields are the same data types and both tables belong to the same database.

Enforcing referential integrity controls the updating of primary key data in the primary table and the deletion of any record from the primary table, if a related record exists elsewhere. A record cannot be added to a related table if a record does not exist in the primary table, e.g. there can be no repair record for a computer unless an associated computer record exists in the primary table.

☜ Manoeuvres

1. Open the **Custom Computers** database and click on the **Relationships** button, to display the relationships.

2. Right click with the mouse on the relationship line between **Computers** and **Repairs** and select **Edit Relationship** from the menu.

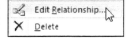

3. In the **Edit Relationship** dialog box, check the box for **Enforce Referential Integrity**.

4. Click **OK**.

continued over

Driving Lesson 29 - Continued

i *Enforcing referential integrity will change the relationship line to show the type of relationship, in this case, one to many.*

5. Close the **Relationships** window.

6. Open the **Computers** table in **Datasheet View**.

7. Click to select the whole record **T2457** and click **✕ Delete ▾** from the **Records** group on the **Home** tab. The record cannot be deleted, as there are related records in the **Repairs** table.

Microsoft Access

⚠ The record cannot be deleted or changed because table 'Repairs' includes related records.

OK   Help

8. Click **OK**. Close the table.

9. Open the **Repairs** table in **Datasheet View**.

10. Click in the empty record row at the end of the table and enter the following information:

18, David, Renew Case, XY33, 29/06/2008

11. Press **<Enter>** after the last entry. As there is no serial number for this job in the **Computers** table, a new job record cannot be created.

Microsoft Access

⚠ You cannot add or change a record because a related record is required in table 'Computers'.

OK   Help

12. Click **OK**. Delete the information just entered using **Undo**.

13. Close the table and leave the database open for the next Driving Lesson

Driving Lesson 30 - Cascade Options

▣ Park and Read

Enforcing referential integrity prevents the deletion or amending of records that would cause related tables to lose integrity. If **Cascade** options are set however, such deletions and amendments <u>are</u> allowed, but related tables will be automatically adjusted. Records in related tables will be automatically deleted or amended.

Manoeuvres

1. The **Custom Computers** database should be open from the previous Driving Lesson.

2. To allow editing or deletion of records, the relationship between the tables must be changed. Click on the **Relationships** button.

3. Right click on the linking line between **Computers** and **Repairs** and select **Edit Relationship**.

4. Edit the relationship as follows: check the boxes for **Cascade Update Related Fields** and **Cascade Delete Related Records**.

5. Click **OK**. This means that any changes made in one related table will be reflected in the others.

6. Close the **Relationships** window.

7. Open the **Computers** table in **Datasheet View** and delete the record for the **Registry Gigathon, R65488G**. This computer has a repair record on the **Repairs** table, record **15**.

continued over

Driving Lesson 30 - Continued

8. Deletion is now allowed but the **Cascade Delete Related Records** option means that the related records (in the **Repairs** table) will also be deleted.

9. Select **Yes** to continue.

*Clicking **No** would cancel the original deletion.*

10. In the **Computers** table, change the serial number **T2457** to **T5724**.

11. Close the table and open the **Repairs** table in **Datasheet View**. The **Cascade Delete Related Records** option has caused the job for the **Registry Gigathon** (job 15) to be automatically removed.

12. Look at the jobs associated with the **Triton** computer (jobs 1, 7 and 14). The **Cascade Update Related Records** option has caused the serial number for these jobs to be automatically amended.

13. Close the table and the database.

Driving Lesson 31 - Revision

This is not an ECDL test. Testing may only be carried out through certified ECDL test centres. This covers the features introduced in this section. Try not to refer to the preceding Driving Lessons while completing it.

1.   Open the **Organiser** database.

2.   In the **Meetings** table add a **Primary Key** to the **Meeting ID** field.

3.   In the **People** table add a **Primary Key** to the **Contact ID** field.

4.   Create a **One to Many** relationship between the tables using the **Contact ID** field.

5.   Enforce **Referential Integrity**, with no **Cascade** options.

6.   Display the **People** table. Use the subdatasheet view to see how many meetings **Ian Chapman** has recorded.

7.   On the same display change the **Contact ID** for **James Tebb** to **KT**. Try to update the record. Why is the update not allowed?

8.   Close all tables, redisplay the relationship between the tables and enforce **Cascade Update Fields** and **Cascade Delete Related Records**.

9.   Change the **Contact ID** for **James Tebb** to **KT** again. Is the update allowed now?

10. In the **Meetings** table change the **Contact ID** field in record 5 from **GS** to **AS** and try to update the record. Why is it still not allowed?

11. Undo the last key stroke then close the table without saving any changes.

12. Close the database.

 *Answers are shown in the **Answers** section at the end of this guide.*

If you experienced any difficulty completing the Revision, refer back to the Driving Lessons in this section. Then redo the Revision.

Driving Lesson 32 - Revision

This is not an ECDL test. Testing may only be carried out through certified ECDL test centres. This covers the features introduced in this section. Try not to refer to the preceding Driving Lessons while completing it.

1. Open the database **Brief Encounter**, a database for an introduction agency.

2. Open the table **Personal records** and scroll to the field **Referred by**. This uses the **BE Number** to indicate who might have referred this client.

3. Design a query that will show the name, rather than the number, of the person referring the client.

4. Show the **First Name** and **Surname** of the client and the **Surname** of the referee.

5. Change the **Caption** of this last field to **Personally referred by** and apply a **Sort** (ascending) to it.

6. Save the query as **Referrals**.

7. Use the same database to create a query showing which men have had introductions.

8. Display the **Surname** and **First Name** fields from the **Personal Records** table and the **Date of Encounter** and **Dating Number** from the **Encounters** table. Include, without displaying, any other fields that may be necessary.

9. Make sure the result will only show men.

10. Check that the join type is **inner** and run the query.

11. How many introductions are there?

12. Save the query as **Introduction**.

13. Use the same query grid to show all introductions by **Surname**, regardless of gender and include those surnames that are yet to receive an introduction (change the type of join). How many records are shown?

14. Save the query as **Dates** then close the query and the database.

i *Answers are shown in the **Answers** section at the end of this guide.*

If you experienced any difficulty completing the Revision, refer back to the Driving Lessons in this section. Then redo the Revision.

Once you are confident with the features, complete the Record of Achievement Matrix referring to the section at the end of the guide. Only when competent move on to the next Section.

Section 5
Forms

By the end of this Section you should be able to:

        Create Sub Forms using a Wizard

        Create Sub Forms Manually

        Link Forms

To gain an understanding of the above features, work through the **Driving Lessons** in this **Section**.

For each **Driving Lesson**, read the **Park and Read** instructions, without touching the keyboard, then work through the numbered steps of the **Manoeuvres** on the computer. Complete the **Revision Exercise(s)** at the end of the section to test your knowledge.

Driving Lesson 33 - Main/Subform: Form Wizard

Park and Read

Just as a subdatasheet can be contained within a datasheet, a subform, containing specific, linked information, can be contained on a main form.

The easiest way to create a **Main/Subform** is to use the **Form Wizard**. A number of questions are then asked, which guide the user through the steps of creating a form with a subform.

Manoeuvres

1. Open the **Contacts** database. Select the **Create** tab and click
    | Form Wizard | in the **Forms** group.

2. The wizard first needs to know which fields are to be used on the main form. From the **Tables/Queries** box, select the table **People**.

3. In the **Available Fields** box, select **Surname** then click on the [>] button to move the field to the **Selected Fields** box. Continue moving all of the fields apart from **Contact ID**, which is not needed on the form.

ℹ️ *Double clicking on the field names in the **Available Fields** box, will place them in the **Selected Fields** box.*

continued over

Driving Lesson 33 - Continued

4. Change the **Tables/Queries** box to show the table **Meetings**. This table will supply the fields for the subform.

5. From the **Available Fields** box, move **Date**, **Subject**, **Discussed** and **Next Contact** to the **Selected Fields** box.

6. Click **Next**. Select to view your data **by People** and ensure **Form with subform(s)** is selected, and then click **Next**.

7. Select a **Datasheet** layout for the subform then click **Next**.

8. The two forms may then be given titles, if required. Leave the titles as they are and click **Finish**. The new form will now appear. Maximise the window if required.

Record Navigation Buttons Subform

Record Navigation Buttons Main form

ℹ️ *As the wizard has been used to setup both the main and the subform, some objects may need to be resized in **Design View** so all the data can be seen. For example, in the picture above, the whole subform area has been moved and adjusted.*

9. The **Main form** contains details of each person, and details of the **Meetings** for that person appear in the **Subform**.

10. Use the main form record navigation buttons at the bottom of the form, to browse through the records of each person. Notice as the person changes in the main form, the meetings details change in the **Subform**.

11. Use the subform navigation buttons to move through the different meetings for each person.

12. Close the form. If prompted, to save, select **Yes** and then close the database.

Driving Lesson 34 - Main/Subform: Subform Wizard

▣ Park and Read

A **Main/Subform** can be created from two existing forms without using the **Form Wizard**. Create both forms in the normal way. Choose one as the main form, and use the **Subform/Subreport** button to add the other as a subform.

⌒ Manoeuvres

1. Open the **Computer Shop** database. There are two forms already created, a **Computer Data Entry** form, which will be the main form, and a **Repairs Subform,** which will become the subform.

2. Open the **Computer Data Entry** form in **Design View**. On the **Design** tab, expand the **Controls** group to display all the buttons by clicking **More,** ⬚.

3. Make sure the **Use Control Wizards** option is turned **on**, ⬚ Use Control Wizards. Click the option if necessary.

4. Click on the **Subform/Subreport** button ⬚ in the expanded **Controls Group**. Position the mouse under the **Address** field and click once.

5. When the **Subform Wizard** appears, choose the **Use an existing form** option and from the list ensure **Repairs Subform** is highlighted.

6. Click **Next**.

continued over

Driving Lesson 34 - Continued

7.   Select to **Choose from a list** and **Show Repairs for each record in Computers using Serial Number**.

8.   Click **Next**. The name for the subform is **Repairs Subform**.

9.   Click **Finish** to create the subform.

10. Save the form and switch to **Form View.** Maximise the window if required.

11. Move through the computer records using the **Record Navigation** buttons at the bottom of the screen. Make sure record **T2457** is displayed. Using the **Subform Navigation** buttons, move through the jobs for this computer.

12. Switch to **Design View** to resize the subform if necessary, so the screen looks like the picture below. Return to **Form View** to check this out.

13. Save and close the form and database.

Driving Lesson 35 - Main/Subform: Manual

▣ Park and Read

The **Main/Subform** can be created without using any wizards. With the main form in **Design View**, and the **Control Wizards** turned **off**, click on the **Subform/Subreport** button. The subform can then be manually added to the main form, and the links and design changed as necessary.

⌒ Manoeuvres

1. Open the **CiA** database. Open the **Orders** form in **Design View**. If the grid is not displayed, right click on a blank area of the form and select **Grid**.

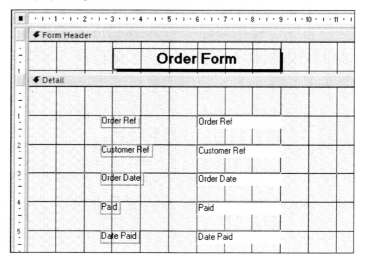

2. Ensure the **Design** tab is displayed, expand the **Controls** options and make sure that the **Use Control Wizards** option is turned **off**, ⚡ Use Control Wizards.

3. Click on the **Subform/Subreport** button, 🖳, and click on the form under **Date Paid**.

4. A box appears with the word Unbound in it, meaning it is not linked to a particular field containing data. This is where the subform will appear, when defined. The size of this box will be changed in the following steps.

5. On the **Design** tab, click the **Property Sheet** button in the **Tools** group to view the **Property Sheet** for the subform. Ensure the **All** tab is selected.

continued over

Driving Lesson 35 - Continued

 *The Name **Child13** may be different on your screen but will still be correct.*

6. Click in the **Source Object** property and from the drop down arrow, choose **Form.Order Details**. This is the table that is the **Source** of the information for the subform.

7. Ensure **Order Ref** appears in **Link Child Fields** and **Link Master Fields**.

 In order to make a main/subform, there must be a linking field in each table so the information in one table can pull out the correct information in the other.

8. Close the **Property Sheet**. Delete the **Child13** label and resize the subform so it is about **7cm** wide and **3cm** deep.

9. Save the form and switch to **Form View**. Browse through the customers. Notice that the orders list in the subform changes to show the details relevant to the viewed customer.

10. Any subform can be deleted from a form. Switch to **Design View** and click on the subform to select it.

 Make sure the subform has handles around it to show it is selected.

11. Press <**Delete**> to remove the subform.

12. Save the form and close it, then close the database.

Driving Lesson 36 - Linking Forms

▣ Park and Read

Instead of creating a form with a subform within it, it is possible to create two forms which are separate, but which link together. The main form will be viewed and when a record is chosen, a button can be pressed which will open up the linked form where the relevant related data will be displayed. This approach is very useful when the main form contains a large amount of information, and the addition of a subform would clutter the screen.

🗘 Manoeuvres

1. Open the **Contacts** database. If there is a **Security Warning** displayed, select **Enable Content** to allow this feature to work.

2. Select the **Create** tab and click 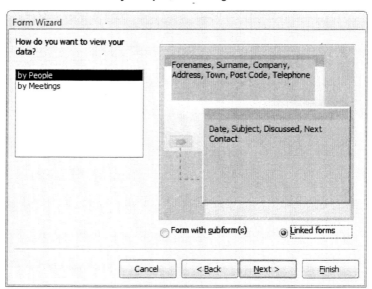 from the **Forms** group.

3. From the **People** table, add all of the fields apart from **Contact ID**.

4. From the **Meetings** table, add all of the fields except the two **ID** fields.

5. Click **Next**.

6. Select to view the data **by People**, and using **Linked forms**.

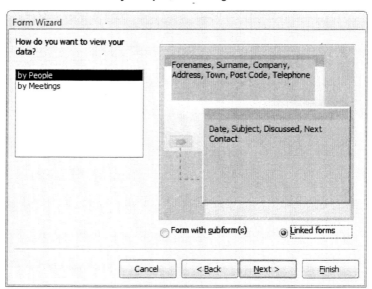

7. Click **Next**.

continued over

Driving Lesson 36 - Continued

8.   Enter a title of **People Linked** for the first form, **Meetings** for the second.

9.   Click **Finish**. The form appears.

[i] *If Access creates a form title which obscures the button, switch to **Design View** and drag the title to the right.*

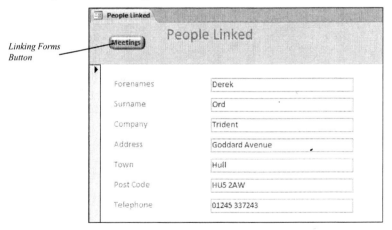

Linking Forms Button

10.   Select record number **6** and click on the **Meetings** button to open up the linked form under another tab. The **Meetings** form may need reformatting.

11.   Display the **People Linked** form again and select another record. The records displayed in the linked **Meetings** form also change.

12.   Close both forms, saving if prompted, and then close the database.

Driving Lesson 37 - Revision

This is not an ECDL test. Testing may only be carried out through certified ECDL test centres. This covers the features introduced in this section. Try not to refer to the preceding Driving Lessons while completing it.

1.　Open the **Custom Computers** database. If the **Computers** and **Repairs** tables are not already linked, do it now.

2.　Create 2 new forms using **Form Design**. The first form is to be the main form, based on the **Computers** table. Save it as **Sandstone Computers**. Do not let *Access 2010* design the form because it may attempt to create the main form/subform automatically.

3.　The second form is to become the subform, based on all the fields from the **Repairs** table. Save it as **Sandstone Repairs**.

4.　Open **Sandstone Computers** and add a subform based on **Sandstone Repairs** to have a similar layout to the form below:

5.　Save the form as **Sandstone Computers** and close it.

6.　Create a query containing all the fields from both the **Computers** and **Repairs** tables but with only one **Serial Number**. Save the query as **Linked**.

7.　Create a simple form based on the **Linked** query. Save it as **Multitable**.

8.　The **Multitable** form navigation buttons show more records than the **Sandstone Computers**. Why is this?

9.　Close the forms and database.

*See the **Answers** section at the back of the guide.*

If you experienced any difficulty completing the Revision, refer back to the Driving Lessons in this section. Then redo the Revision.

Driving Lesson 38 - Revision

This covers the features introduced in this section. Try not to refer to the preceding Driving Lessons while completing it.

1.   Open the database **Brief Encounter**.

2.   Create a form with a subform for the two tables using any method (the main form is to be based on **Personal records**).

3.   Save the forms as **Introduction** and **Introduction Subform**.

4.   Edit the form so that all fields in the subform are displayed (it may be necessary to widen the form area).

5.   Use the main form to find record **6** (Philip Baron).

6.   Enter records on the subform to record meetings with **Henrietta Potts** and **Beryl Barrington**.

7.   Close the form and the database.

If you experienced any difficulty completing the Revision, refer back to the Driving Lessons in this section. Then redo the Revision.

Once you are confident with the features, complete the Record of Achievement Matrix referring to the section at the end of the guide. Only when competent move on to the next Section.

Section 6
Form Controls

By the end of this Section you should be able to:

Create the following controls:

> **Calculated Fields on Forms**
>
> **Command Buttons**
>
> **Combo Boxes**
>
> **List Boxes and Check Boxes**
>
> **Option Groups**
>
> **Add Data Fields to Headers and Footers**

To gain an understanding of the above features, work through the **Driving Lessons** in this **Section**.

For each **Driving Lesson**, read the **Park and Read** instructions, without touching the keyboard, then work through the numbered steps of the **Manoeuvres** on the computer. Complete the **Revision Exercise(s)** at the end of the section to test your knowledge.

Driving Lesson 39 - Calculated Fields: Forms

▣ Park and Read

There are different types of form controls: **bound** (gets its data from a source/field) **unbound** (not linked to a data source) and **calculated**. A calculated field uses a mathematical expression to obtain its information. These fields are calculated using other information from the database and are calculated each time they are required.

The calculation is entered into a text box. The expression may include any of the usual mathematical symbols (+ - * /) and expressions such as **Average**, **Sum**, **Max** and **Min**. When the form is viewed, the field will calculate the expression, and will recalculate as the record changes.

↷ Manoeuvres

1. Open the **Pets** database and the **Pet Entry Form** in **Form View**. A calculated field is to be created to calculate the total value of sales for each pet, based on the price multiplied by the quantity sold.

2. Switch to **Design View** and click on the **Text Box** button in the **Controls** group of the **Design** tab. Click below the **Number Sold** field on the form. An **unbound** control is created (not linked to data source). Click away from the new field to see it correctly.

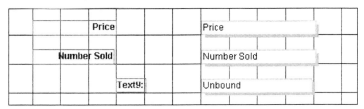

3. Display the **Property Sheet** for the new field, select the **Data** tab and click the **Control Source** drop down arrow. Select **Animal** from the list. The field is now a **Bound** text box.

ℹ️ *All fields added to a form by dragging from the field list are in **Bound** text boxes.*

4. The field can be modified by changing any **Property Sheet** settings, but for now close the **Property Sheet** and press <Delete> to remove the field.

5. Add a new unbound text box in the same position and enter the following expression:

    =[Price]*[Number Sold]

ℹ️ *Any field names used must be entered within square brackets.*

continued over

Driving Lesson 39 - Continued

6. Click on the label next to the calculated field, delete the text and enter **Total Amount**. Resize and reposition the label and field if necessary.

Number Sold			Number Sold	
Total Amount			=[Price]*[Number Sold]	

7. Display the **Property Sheet** for the calculated field, select its **Format** tab and click the drop down arrow in **Format**. Select **Currency**.

8. Select the **Other** tab in the **Property Sheet** and change the **Name** from **Text9** (or similar) to **Amount**.

9. Switch to **Form View** to see the result.

10. Switch back to **Design View** with the **Design** tab selected. Add another **Text Box** below the new one. Enter the following expression:

   =IIf([Amount]>50,"High Value","Low Value")

 *This logical expression displays one of two messages, depending on the value of the calculated **Amount** field.*

11. Click on the label for the new field and delete it (be careful not to delete the field).

12. Switch to **Form View**. A calculation appears which is the **Price** multiplied by the **Number Sold**, with a text message below it.

Price	£30.00
Number Sold	3
Total Amount	£90.00
	High Value

13. View the next record - the new **Total Amount** is automatically calculated.

14. Change the **Number Sold** in record **2** to **100**, then click in the **Total Amount** field. The figure is recalculated.

15. Switch to **Design View**. Change the **Total Amount** calculation to **=[Price]*[Number Sold]*0.9**. Change the label to **Discounted Amount**.

16. Click on the text box with the **=IIf** calculation field and press **<Delete>**.

17. Switch to **Form View** to see the effect.

18. Save and close the form and close the database.

Driving Lesson 40 - Combo Box 1: Wizard

▣ Park and Read

A **Combo Box** is a field on a form, which will allow a value to be chosen from a drop down list or will allow a value to be entered (unless restricted by the field properties). This will speed up data entry and will stop incorrect data entry, such as spelling mistakes, etc.

There are three options to choose from, when using the wizard:

I want the combo box to look up the values in a table or query

The combo box will display the values already in a specified field in a named table. The default is to show all values, even when there are duplicates.

I will type in the values that I want

The combo box will display the values that have been typed into a list when the box was created. Values can be amended later in the field properties.

Find a record on my form based on the value I selected in my combo box

The combo box will display the values from a field in the current table. The value selected will be used to search for a record that matches the entry. It is advisable to use a field unique to each record, such as a reference number.

The following Driving Lessons cover creating a combo box using each of the options.

⟲ Manoeuvres

1. Open the **Authors** database and the **English Literature** form in **Design View**.

2. Select the **Surname** label and field and press <**Delete**> to remove both.

3. Instead of just typing an entry in **Surname**, a **Combo Box** will be used to give the option of selecting any value of surname already in the table. Ensure the **Use Control Wizards** option is turned **on**.

4. From the **Controls** group, click on the **Combo Box** button ⊞ . Place the cursor where the **Surname** field was and click once to create the combo box.

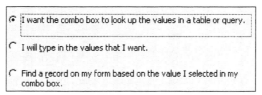

continued over

Driving Lesson 40 - Continued

5. Select the first option, **I want the combo box to look up the values in a table or query**. Click **Next**.

6. The table, which contains the values to appear in the combo box, is the **Author** table. Select **Author** from the list of tables.

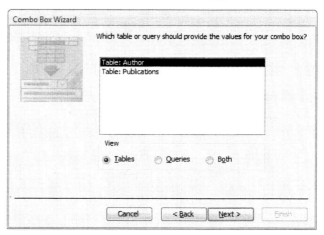

7. Click **Next**. It is the **Author Name** field that contains the values to appear in the combo box. Select **Author Name** and click ⌐ > ⌐.

8. Click **Next**. There is no need for a sort so click **Next** again. If necessary resize the column so all information is displayed, then click **Next**.

9. Once a value has been chosen from the combo box, it needs to be stored in the **Surname** field on the table. Select **Store that value in this field** and choose the **Surname** field.

continued over

Driving Lesson 40 - Continued

10. Click **Next**. Enter **Surname** as the label for the combo box. Click **Finish**.

11. Click in the **First Name** field. Click on the **Format Painter** button , on the **Home** tab, then click on the **Surname** field to copy the same format from the **First Name** field, to the **Surname** field.

12. Resize and reposition the **Surname** field as appropriate.

13. Because the combo box for **Surname** was added last, it is automatically positioned at the bottom of the tab order list, which governs the way the cursor moves around the form when tab is pressed. To move it up the tab order sequence, display the **Design** tab and click the **Tab Order** button.

14. Click the **Auto Order** button in the **Tab Order** dialog box to make the tab order the same as the order of fields on the form, i.e. top field first. Note that fields can be dragged up and down the list to produce any tab order required.

15. Click **OK** then save the form and switch to **Form View**.

16. Click on the **New Record** button at the bottom of the screen.

17. Click the drop down arrow on the **Surname** box and select **Austen** from the list.

[i] *As this is a **Combo** field, it is possible to type in a value instead.*

18. Complete the remaining fields exactly as shown below and press <**Enter**>.

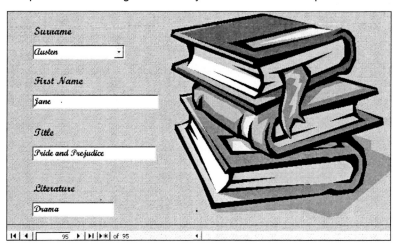

19. Leave the form open for the next Driving Lesson.

Driving Lesson 41 - Limit to List

▣ Park and Read

By default it is possible to type any value in a combo box, but this can be changed.

⎘ Manoeuvres

1.　Ensure the **English Literature** form is open and in **Form View** with a blank new record screen displayed.

2.　Click in the **Surname** field and type **Barnacle**. Press **<Enter>**. Even though this is not a value on the **Author** table it is still accepted.

3.　Click the **Undo** button to reverse the entry.

4.　Switch to **Design View** and display the **Property Sheet** for the **Surname** combo box field.

5.　Select the **Data** tab for the **Property Sheet** and change the **Limit To List** setting to **Yes**.

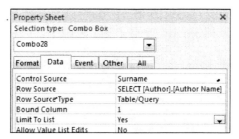

6.　Close the **Property Sheet** and switch to **Datasheet View**.

7.　Click on the **New Record** button at the bottom of the screen then click in the **Surname** field and type **Barnacle**. Press **<Enter>**. Now the entry will not be accepted because it is not on the **Author** table.

8.　Click **OK** to the message then click **Undo**. Switch to **Design View**.

9.　Select the **Surname** combo box field and press **<Delete>**. The field is removed.

10.　Click **Add Existing Fields** from the **Design** tab to display the **Field List** and drag the **Surname** field from the list back to its original position on the form.

11.　Use **Format Painter** to copy the same format from the **First Name** field to the **Surname** field.

12.　Save the form and leave it open for the next exercise.

Driving Lesson 42 - Combo Box 2: Wizard

▣ Park and Read

For a small number of values in a combo box it may be easier to look up a separate list, entered as part of the setting up process for the box itself.

⌁ Manoeuvres

1. Ensure the **English Literature** form is open and in **Design View**.

2. Remove the **Literature** label and field. Ensure the **Use Control Wizards** option is turned **on**. Click the **Combo Box** button, ▦ and click once below the **Title** field.

3. From the wizard select the second option, **I will type in the values that I want**. Click **Next**.

4. Specify that **1** column is required in the combo box and enter these following values, pressing **Tab** after each entry: **Prosy** (incorrectly spelt) **Drama** and **Poetry**.

5. Click **Next**. Select to **Store that value in this field** and select the **Literature** field.

6. Click **Next**. Enter **Literature** as the label and click **Finish**.

7. Resize the combo box and label as appropriate. Format it in the same way as the other fields.

8. There has been a spelling mistake in the combo box. To change values in a combo box, select the combo box and view its **Property Sheet**. Select the **Data** tab and then select the **Row Source** property.

9. Use the ←→ keys to navigate to the **Prosy** entry, change the spelling to **Prose**.

10. From the **Limit to List** property, select **Yes**. This means that users will not be able to enter any other text; just to select from the combo box.

11. Close the **Property Sheet** and save the form.

12. Switch to **Form View** and move to record number **95**. Using the new combo box, change the literature field from **Drama** to **Prose**.

13. Leave the form and database open for the next Driving Lesson.

Driving Lesson 43 - Combo Box 3: Wizard

Park and Read

A combo box can be used to find a value from the current table and use that to retrieve the appropriate record. When creating these combo boxes, it is better to include the **Primary Key** as the field in the combo box, as this is a unique field in the table and each value will successfully locate a single record.

Manoeuvres

1. With the **English Literature** form open from the previous Driving Lesson, switch to **Design View**.

2. Ensure the **Use Control Wizards** option is turned **on**. Click the **Combo Box** button, and click once in the **Form Header**.

3. From the wizard select **Find a record on my form...** Click **Next**.

4. Double click on **Title** to move it to **Selected Fields**. This is the field that will be searched by the combo box, to display the desired record.

5. Click **Next**. Resize the **Title** field if necessary.

6. Click **Next** and change the **Label** text to **Title Search**.

7. Click **Finish**. Copy the format of the other fields to the new field using the **Format Painter** and reposition/resize as required. Save the form and switch to **Form View**.

8. Click on the **Combo Box** drop down arrow in the **Form Header**. A list of all the publication titles on the table appears.

9. Select any title from the list to display all the fields from the desired record. Do not select a title containing an apostrophe, the *Access* process cannot handle this without amendment to the underlying code.

10. Close the form and close the database.

Driving Lesson 44 - Combo Box: Manual

▣ Park and Read

Combo boxes can be created without using a wizard. A combo box can be placed on to the form with the **Control Wizards** feature turned **off**. The properties of the combo box will be set up separately.

Manoeuvres

1. Open the **Premises** database and open the **New Premises** form. This is a form to add new premises to the table. The form is going to have a combo box added manually to select a location from a list of those used already.

2. Switch to **Design View** and delete the **Location** field and label.

3. Switch **off** the **Use Control Wizards** option, and use the **Combo Box** button, ⊞, to create a combo box in the space just created.

4. Display the **Property Sheet** for the combo box selecting the **All** tab to view all the properties.

5. Click in the **Row Source** property and click on the **Build** button ⊡. The **Show Table** dialog box and **Query Builder** window appear.

6. Select the **Commercial** table from the **Show Table** dialog box. Click **Add** then **Close**. Add the **Location** field to the query grid.

7. Close the **Query Builder** selecting **Yes** to save the changes. An expression appears in the **Row Source** property.

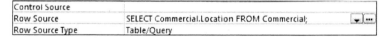

Control Source	
Row Source	SELECT Commercial.Location FROM Commercial;
Row Source Type	Table/Query

8. Change the combo box label to **Area** and if necessary use **Format Painter** to make sure the field matches others on the form.

9. Switch to **Form View** and click the drop down arrow in the **Area** field. All the current locations are listed but there is a lot of duplication.

continued over

Driving Lesson 44 - Continued

10. Switch back to **Design View** and display the **Property Sheet** for the **Area** field.

11. Click in the **Row Source** property and click on the **Build** button 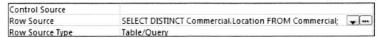. The **Query Builder** window appears.

12. Click in a blank area of the **Query Builder** window so that the **Property Sheet** shows details of the query.

13. Set the **Unique Values** property to **Yes**. This selects only **Distinct** values, i.e. it will stop any duplicate values being shown in the combo box.

14. Close the **Query Builder** selecting **Yes** to save the changes. The expression in the **Row Source** property has changed.

Control Source	
Row Source	SELECT DISTINCT Commercial.Location FROM Commercial;
Row Source Type	Table/Query

*Increase the size of the dialog box if all the **Row Source** cannot be seen.*

15. Select the **Control Source** property and from the drop down list choose **Location**. This stores information from the **Combo Box** into the **Location** field. The field therefore is now defined as a **Bound Control**.

16. Move the new combo box field to second in the **Tab Order** list (below **Property Ref**) by using the **Tab Order** function from the from the **Design** tab.

17. Save the form as **New Premises 2** and switch to **Form View**.

18. Create a new record (Ref **P022**) and click the drop down.arrow in the **Area** combo box. All existing values are shown, but now only once each.

19. Select **DockLand**. Complete the rest of the fields on the form.

20. Close the form but not the database.

Driving Lesson 45 - List Boxes

▣ Park and Read

List Boxes are similar to combo boxes except the options are permanently viewed in a list format, and no manual entry is allowed. The amount of values which appear in the box depends on the size of the list box you create. If the list box is too small, scroll bars will appear to the side of the list box, to allow you to scroll through the values.

Manoeuvres

1. With the **Premises** database open from the previous Driving Lesson, open the original **New Premises** form in **Design View**.

2. Ensure the **Use Control Wizards** option is turned <u>on</u>. Delete the **Glazing** field in the **Detail** section of the form.

3. Select the **List Box** button and click once where the **Glazing** field used to be. The **List Box Wizard** appears.

4. Notice that the options for a list box are exactly the same as for a combo box. Select **I will type in the values...** and click **Next**.

5. Type in **None**, **Standard**, **Tinted** and **Double**, using <Tab> to move to a new line after each entry.

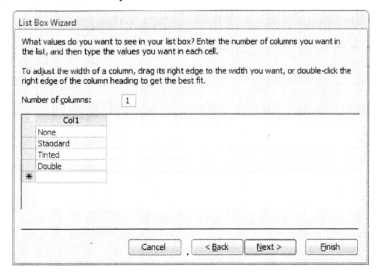

6. Click **Next**, choose **Store that value in this field** and select the **Glazing** field. Click **Next**.

continued over

Driving Lesson 45 - Continued

7.   Enter the label as **Glazing** and click **Finish**.

8.   Use **Format Painter** to standardise the appearance of the new field if necessary, then reposition/resize the field until the form has a similar layout to the diagram below.

9.   Save the form and switch to **Form View**. Make sure the record for **M001** is displayed.

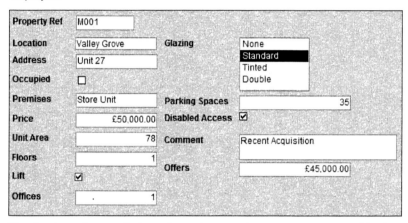

10. The list box shows all the values that can be entered into the **Glazing** field. The value for the current record is the one that is highlighted.

11. To change the value for the record on the screen, click on **Double**.

12. Start a new record and notice that nothing is selected in **Glazing** by default.

13. Switch to **Design View** and view the properties for the list box. On the **Data** tab, enter **Standard** in the **Default Value** property.

14. Switch to **Form View** and start a new record. Notice now that **Standard** is selected in the **Glazing** field.

15. Switch to **Design View** and decrease the depth of the **Glazing** list box to about half of its current size.

16. Return to **Form View**. The list box should now require scroll bars to enable all the available values to be viewed.

17. Save the form and leave it and the database open for the next Driving Lesson.

Driving Lesson 46 - Check Boxes

▣ Park and Read

Check box controls can be added to forms when a **Yes/No** type of answer is required, i.e. check the box for **Yes**.

↰ Manoeuvres

1. Display the **New Premises** form in **Design View**. The fields **Occupied**, **Lift** and **Disabled Access** are defined in the table as **Yes/No** fields and therefore check boxes have been automatically assigned to them by default when they were included in the form.

2. Close the form and open the **Commercial** table in **Design View**.

3. View the field properties for the **Occupied** field and click the **Lookup** tab.

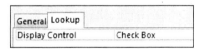

4. The **Display Control** property defines how the field will be displayed and by default it is set to **Check Box** for a **Yes/No** field.

[i] *The alternative display options are **Text Box** or **Combo Box**.*

5. Close the **Commercial** table. Open the **New Premises** form in **Design View**, and make sure the **Use Control Wizards** option is turned <u>on.</u> Click **Add Existing Fields** to display the **Field List**.

6. Drag the **Public Address** field onto the form below the **Offers** field. It appears as a check box.

7. With the check box still selected, press <**Delete**>. The field is removed.

8. Check boxes can be added manually. Select the **Check Box** button, from the expanded **Controls** group and click underneath **Offers**.

9. View the **Property Sheet** for the check box (not the label). Select the **All** tab and change the **Name** to **Public Address**.

10. Click in **Control Source** and click the drop down arrow on the right.

11. Scroll down the list and select the **Public Address** field as the source to be attached to this check box. Close the **Property Sheet**.

12. Change the label to **Public Address**, move it to the left of the check box, then save the form and switch to **Form View**.

13. Close the form and the database.

Driving Lesson 47 - Option Groups

▣ Park and Read

Option Groups allow a selection to be made from a number of option buttons.
Only one option can be chosen from any group.

Manoeuvres

1. Open the **Authors** database and the **English Literature** form in **Design View**.

2. Ensure the **Design** tab is selected and the **Use Control Wizards** option is turned **on**.

3. Delete the **Literature** combo box from the form.

4. Click the **Option Group** button, ⌐**XYZ**⌐, Click on the form where the field has been deleted. The **Option Group Wizard** appears.

5. In **Label Names**, enter **Drama**, press <Tab>, then enter **Prose**, <Tab>, and finally **Poetry**.

6. Click **Next**.

7. There is no default choice so select **No I don't want a default**. Click **Next**.

8. This dialog box specifies the values that are to be assigned to the choices. Using an option group means that instead of storing actual text on the table, all that is stored is a number representing the choice, e.g. the field in the table will contain **1** instead of **Drama**, **2** instead of **Prose** and **3** instead of **Poetry**. Click **Next** to accept these defaults.

continued over

Driving Lesson 47 - Continued

9.   Specify to **Store this value in this field** and select the **Literature** field. Click **Next**.

10. This dialog box specifies the type of buttons and style that are to be used. Select the different buttons and styles to see the effect.

11. Choose **Option buttons** and the **Style** as **Shadowed**.

12. Click **Next**. Enter **Classification** as the caption for the option group and click **Finish**.

13. Use **Format Painter** to standardize the appearance of the option group captions, then resize/reposition where necessary. Save the form and switch to **Form View**.

14. View the first record. Click **Poetry** to set this option for the first record. Set records **2** and **3** as **Prose**.

15. Open the **Publications** table to see how this has affected values in the **Literature** column. Note that only data processed through the form is affected, other records are unchanged. Close the table.

16. With the **English Literature** form displayed, switch to **Design View**.

17. Click the edge of the **Option Group** to select it. Display the properties.

i   *Make sure the whole group is selected, not just an individual button or label. The **Name** as shown in the **Properties** box should be **Frame28** or similar.*

18. Select the **Format** tab and change the **Special Effect** to **Sunken**.

i   *With the option group selected, pressing <**Delete**> would remove the whole group and contents.*

19. Switch to **Form View** to see the effect then save the form, close it, and close the database.

Driving Lesson 48 - Form Headers and Footers

▣ Park and Read

Forms can have Header and Footer areas defined which appear at the beginning and end of every form. Page Headers and Footers are only seen when the forms are printed and appear at the top and bottom of every printed page. Data fields can be added to header and footer areas. These can include fields from the field list or the date and time.

⌒ Manoeuvres

1. Open the **Premises** database and open the **New Premises** form in **Design View**. Right click on a blank area of the form and select

   ▦   Form H̲eader/Footer

2. The form now has two new areas, a **Form Header** area above the **Detail** and a **Form Footer** area below. Drag the **Address** field from the field list to the centre of the **Form Header** area. Change the label text to **Property**.

3. To insert the date, make sure the **Design** tab is displayed and click the **Date and Time** button, 📅, in the **Header/Footer** group.

4. In the **Date and Time** dialog box, remove the check from **Include Time**.

5. Leave all other settings and click **OK**. The date is inserted as a field.

6. Switch to **Form View** to see the actual date which appears at the top of every form.

7. Close the form, saving if prompted, then close the database.

Driving Lesson 49 - Command Button: Wizard

▣ Park and Read

A **Command Button** is a control on a form which can be clicked to perform an action, such as closing forms, opening reports, printing, etc.

An easy way to define a command button is to use the **Command Button Wizard**, which takes the user through the steps of creating a button.

⌒ Manoeuvres

1. Open the **Pets** database and open the **Pet Entry Form** in **Design View**. Click and drag the bottom edge of the **Form Footer** area to expand it.

2. Ensure the **Design** tab is displayed and **Use Control Wizards** option is turned <u>on</u>.

3. Click on **Button**, ⬚, from the **Controls** group, and click once on the left side of the **Form Footer** to create a button.

4. In the **Command Button Wizard** dialog box, click on the different **Categories** and view what **Actions** can be applied to a command button.

5. Select **Record Operations** from **Categories** and **Add New Record** from **Actions**.

6. Click **Next**. This screen defines how the button will appear on the form. Select the **Text**, option, press <Tab> and enter the text: **New Record**.

7. Click **Next**. The button now needs to be given a name, so that it can be referred to later. Call the button **Add New** then click **Finish**.

8. Switch to **Form View**. Click the **New Record** button to automatically display a new, blank record.

9. Save the form and close the database.

Driving Lesson 50 - Revision

This is not an ECDL test. Testing may only be carried out through certified ECDL test centres. This covers the features introduced in this section. Try not to refer to the preceding Driving Lessons while completing it.

1. Open the **Custom Computers** database.

2. Open the **Repairs Entry** form.

3. Remove the **Serial Number** field and label from the form.

4. Replace it with a **Combo Box** field that will look up values from the **Serial Number** field in the **Computers** table. Store the selected value in the **Serial Number** field in the **Repairs** table. Use **Serial No** as the label for the combo box field.

5. Check that the new field drops down a list of all available serial numbers.

6. Create a command button in the footer of the form. Define the button so that clicking on it will print out a copy of the **Repairs** table. This option is in the **Miscellaneous** category.

7. Format the button as desired.

8. Switch to **Form View** and test the use of the command button.

9. Save the new form as **New Repairs**.

10. Close the form, then close the database.

If you experienced any difficulty completing the Revision, refer back to the Driving Lessons in this section. Then redo the Revision.

Driving Lesson 51 - Revision

This covers the features introduced in this section. Try not to refer to the
preceding Driving Lessons while completing it.

1. Open the **Houses** database and open the **Data Entry** form in **Design
    View**.

2. Move the **Address** field and the **Location** field into the **Form Header**
    area. Delete the labels for these two fields.

3. In the space left in the **Detail Area**, insert a **List Box** which displays a list
    of typed values: **House, Apartment, Town House**. Store the selected
    value in the **Type of Property** field and name the field **Type**.

4. Adjust the size of the **List Box** to fit the space.

5. Delete the **Bedrooms** field and insert an **Option Group** on the right of the
    form.

6. The **Option Labels** are **One, Two, Three, Four** and **More**, with no
    default.

7. Accept the default values of **1, 2** and **3**, etc. and store the value in the
    Bedrooms field.

8. Set a caption of **Bedrooms**.

9. Save the form and switch to **Form View**.

10. Move to record **5** and change the number of bedrooms to **Four**.

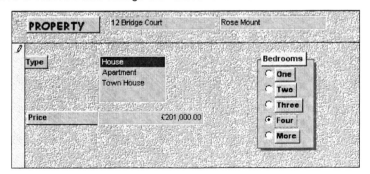

11. Close the form and close the database.

If you experienced any difficulty completing the Revision, refer back to the
Driving Lessons in this section. Then redo the Revision.

Once you are confident with the features, complete the Record of Achievement
Matrix referring to the section at the end of the guide. Only when competent
move on to the next Section.

Section 7
Reports

By the end of this Section you should be able to:

Create Grouped Reports

Create Subreports

Insert Page Breaks

Create Calculated Fields in Reports

Calculate Percentages

Insert Data Fields in Headers and Footers

Print Reports

To gain an understanding of the above features, work through the **Driving Lessons** in this **Section**.

For each **Driving Lesson**, read the **Park and Read** instructions, without touching the keyboard, then work through the numbered steps of the **Manoeuvres** on the computer. Complete the **Revision Exercise(s)** at the end of the section to test your knowledge.

Driving Lesson 52 - Grouped Report: Wizard

🅿 Park and Read

Information within a report can be **grouped**, so that records which contain the same information in a particular field, can appear grouped together on the report. Sorts can also be applied within the groups.

☞ Manoeuvres

1. Open the **Premises** database, display the **Create** tab and click on the **Report Wizard** button, 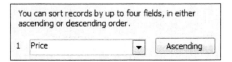.

2. Ensure the **Commercial** table is selected in the **Tables/Queries** box. Select **Location** from **Available Fields** and click **>** to move it into **Selected Fields**. Similarly select **Address, Type of Premises** and **Price**.

3. Click **Next**. The report is to be grouped by **Location**. Select the **Location** field and click on **>** to create the grouping.

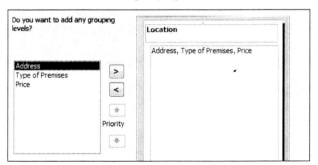

4. Click **Next**. Sort in **Ascending** order of **Price**.

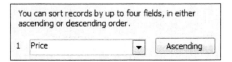

continued over

Driving Lesson 52 - Continued

5. Click 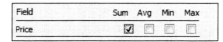 to see a matrix of numeric fields and summary types. Select the option to calculate **Sum** of **Price**.

Field	Sum	Avg	Min	Max
Price	☑	☐	☐	☐

6. Click **OK** then click **Next**.

7. Choose **Stepped Layout** and an orientation of **Landscape**. Click **Next**.

8. Name the report **Grouped Location** and click **Finish** to view the report.

9. The properties are all grouped by **Location** and appear in **Price** order within that location. The **Sum** of prices appears automatically in a special summary area for each **Location**.

10. The report wizard does not always make fields large enough to completely display the data. Close the **Print Preview**, then display the report in **Design View** and enlarge any such fields, making use of any unused space. For example, if necessary, enlarge the **Price** field by dragging the left edge to the left . Switch to **Report View** to see the effect.

Grouped Report		
Location	Price Address	Type of Premises
Central Area		
	£56,000.00 The Lothian Suites	Conference Unit
	£75,000.00 10 Willow Road	Office Premises
	£100,000.00 16 Station Road	Office Premises

11. To make the **Price Sum** field a running total rather than a separate total for each group, switch to **Design View**.

12. Right click the **=Sum([Price])** field in the **Location Footer** and select **Properties** from the shortcut menu.

13. Select the **Data** tab in the **Property Sheet**, click the **Running Sum** property and click the drop down arrow.

14. Select the **Over Group** option and preview the report. The **Price Sum** total field is now cumulative for each group, so that the total value for the last group is the same as the report **Grand Total**.

15. Switch to **Design View** and change the **Running Sum** property for the **Location Footer** total field to **Over All**.

16. Preview the report. The group totals are now cumulative over the whole report, but because there is only one level of grouping the results are the same as before.

17. Close the report, saving any changes, then close the database.

Driving Lesson 53 - Grouped Report: Manual

▣ Park and Read

Grouped reports can also be created without using a wizard.

⌒ Manoeuvres

1. Open the **Contacts** database.

2. Display the **Current Contacts** report in **Print Preview**. This is a simple listing of data from the **Meetings** and **People** tables.

3. Switch to **Design View** and make sure the **Design** tab is displayed.

4. To group the report data, click the **Group & Sort** button, [≣ Group & Sort]. A **Group, Sort and Total** panel opens underneath the **Design** window.

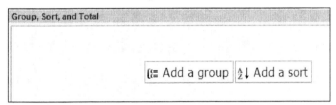

5. Click the **Add a group** button, then select **Subject** from the list of available fields. Notice a new area, **Subject Header**, appears on the form and the grouping structure is shown in the lower panel.

6. Click [More ►] from the group line on the **Group, Sort and Total** panel to see the other options that may be defined for grouping.

7. Click the [with A on top ▼] drop down arrow and select **with Z on top**. The groups (**Subjects**) are sorted in descending alphabetic order.

continued over

Driving Lesson 53 - Continued

8. Click the `without a footer section ▾` drop down arrow and select the option, **with a footer section**. Another new area, **Subject Footer**, appears on the form. Group totals could be defined here.

9. Click the `do not keep group together on one page ▾` drop down arrow and select the option, **keep whole group together on one page**.

10. Click the `↓ᴬᵤ Add a sort` button and select **Company** from the list of available fields. Within each group, records will be sorted alphabetically by company.

11. In **Design View**, move the **Subject** field to the **Subject Header**. Remove the label and increase the **Font Size** of the **Subject** field to **12** and make it **Bold**. Apply a **Special Effect** of **Shadowed** and resize the field if necessary.

12. Save the report as **Grouped Subjects**. Change the view to **Print Preview** to preview the report. Note the number of pages.

13. Look at the first page. All the records for each subject are grouped together. Return to **Design View**.

14. Double click on the bar across the top of the **Subject Header** section to show the **Property Sheet** for this section. Select the **Format** tab of the **Property Sheet** and set the **Force New Page** property to **Before Section** so that each group will start on a new page.

ℹ️ *Page breaks can be forced in any section of a report by selecting the section and setting the **Force New Page** property in the **Property Sheet**.*

15. Close the **Property Sheet** and preview the report again. Notice how each group is on a new page and the number of pages has increased.

16. Close **Print Preview**. Close the report and database, saving any changes.

Driving Lesson 54 - Subreports

▣ Park and Read

Just as a subform can be contained within a main form, a subreport containing specific, linked information, can be contained on a main report.

The easiest way to create a main/subreport is to use the **SubReport Wizard**. A number of questions are then asked to guide you through the steps.

⌒ Manoeuvres

1.   Open the **Transport** database and open the **Bus Details** report.

2.   Switch to **Design View** and increase the height of the **Detail** area.

3.   With the **Control Wizard** on, click **Subform/Subreport**, [⊞] and click in the **Detail** area beneath the existing fields.

4.   From the **SubReport Wizard**, select to **Use an existing report or form** and select the **Servicing History** report.

5.   Click **Next**.

6.   Select to **Choose from a list** and select to **Show Servicing Records for each record in Buses using Fleet Number**.

continued over

Driving Lesson 54 - Continued

7.   Click **Next** and accept the subreport name **Servicing History**.

8.   Click **Finish**, then save and view the report.

  *The column headings in the **Servicing History** report were included in the report header area so that they would be displayed when the report was used as a subreport.*

9.   Switch to **Design View** and select the subreport. Display the **Property Sheet** and check that **Servicing History** is displayed as the selected object.

10. Press <**Delete**> to remove the subreport from the report layout.

11. Close the report <u>without</u> saving and close the database.

Driving Lesson 55 - Calculated Fields: Reports

▣ Park and Read

Summary calculation fields are usually added to reports as part of defining grouping levels, but they can be manually created to obtain any mathematical/statistical information that may be required. Calculations using expressions like **Sum** and **Count** will have different effects depending on where they are added in the report.

⌒ Manoeuvres

1. Open the **Houses** database and open the **Property by Type** report in **Design View**.

2. Display the **Page Setup** tab and click **Landscape** to change the page orientation.

3. Display the **Design** tab and click [≣ Group & Sort] to see that grouping by **Type of Property** has already been defined.

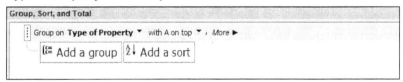

4. Use [More ▶] to expand the options. Change the settings so that the group is shown **with a footer section**.

5. Click on the **Text Box** button, [ab], on the **Design** tab and click in the **Type of Property Footer**. In the **Unbound** box enter the following calculation: **=Count([Address])**. This will count how many properties are in each group.

6. Change the label to **Number of Properties**.

7. Create another **Text Box** in the **Type of Property Footer**, under the previous box. Resize the footer if necessary. Enter the calculation: **=Avg([Price])**. This will calculate the average price of property per group.

8. View the **Avg([Price])** field property and set the **Format** property to **Currency**, **Decimal Places** to **0** and the label to **Average Price**.

continued over

Driving Lesson 55 - Continued

9. To total the price of all properties, create a third text box in the **Type of Property Footer**.

10. Enter the expression: **=Sum([Price])** and set the **Format** property to **Currency**, **Decimal Places** to **0** and the label to **Total Price**.

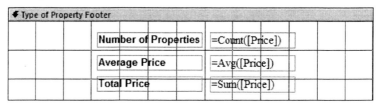

11. Switch to **Print Preview** and scroll through the pages to view the calculations.

12. Return to **Design View**. Click and drag a box around the **Count**, **Avg and Sum** calculated fields to select them. Right click on any of the selected fields and select ⎣🗐 _Copy_ ⎦ from the shortcut menu.

13. Enlarge the **Report Footer** area, right click in it, and select ⎣🗐 _Paste_ ⎦ to paste the fields into the area.

14. Change the field labels in the **Report Footer** to **Total Number of Properties**, **Report Average Price** and **Report Total Price**.

15. Preview the report. At the end of the report are the total number, average price and total price of properties for the entire report.

16. Save and close the report, then close the database.

17. Open the **Computer Shop** database and create a new report in **Design View** using the **Repairs** table as the **Record Source** in the report **Property Sheet**. Place all fields on to the **Detail** area.

18. In the **Page Header** create the label **Maximum and Minimum Costs**. Increase the text size to **12pt bold**.

19. Right click on a blank area of the form and select **Report Header/Footer**.

20. In the **Report Footer** area, create a text box and enter the expression: **=Max([Price])**. In the **Property Sheet**, format the field as **Currency** with **2 Decimal Places**. Change the label to **Maximum Price**.

21. Create a second text box beneath the first and enter the following expression: **=Min([Price])**. Format the field as before and change the label to **Minimum Price**.

continued over

Driving Lesson 55 - Continued

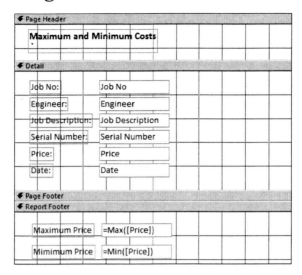

22. Preview the report and scroll to the end to see maximum and minimum costs for all repairs.

23. Save the report as **Max Costs** and close it. Close the database.

24. Calculated fields can also involve text fields. Open the **Staff** database.

25. Open the **Staffing** report in **Design View**. The two name fields can be combined into a single field. This is called **concatenation**.

26. Delete the **Surname** and **First Name** labels and fields.

27. Create a text box above the fields (move them all down if necessary) and enter the following expression: **=[First Name] & " " & [Surname]**. The **&** symbol is known as **concatenate** and the space is added in to separate the fields. Change the label to **Name**.

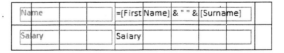

28. Preview the report and notice the names are now shown in a single field.

29. Close the report and the database, saving any changes.

Driving Lesson 56 - Calculating Percentages

▣ Park and Read

Calculated fields can be used to show percentages in reports. In particular they can show the value of each detail line as a percentage of the report total.

⟨ Manoeuvres

1. Open the **Pets** database and the **Percentage Sold** report in **Design View**. This report contains a record for each sale, including the number of animals sold, and a calculated field in the **Report Footer** to show the total number of animals sold. A calculated field can be added to each detail line to show the number sold as a percentage of the total number sold.

2. Click on the calculated **Sum** in the **Report Footer** and display the **Property Sheet**. The name of this control should be **Text12**.

3. Use the **Text Box** button 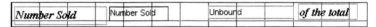 from the **Design** tab to create a new field at the right of the **Number Sold** field in the **Detail** area.

4. Click and drag the new label box to the right of the **Unbound** box and enter the text '**of the total**'. Adjust the positions as shown below.

5. Select the **Unbound** box and click the **Data** tab in the **Property Sheet**.

6. In **Control Source**, enter. the calculation: **=[Number Sold] / [Text12]**.

ℹ *If a report has grouped subtotals, percentages can be calculated as a percentage of the group totals instead of report totals, or they can be placed in the group footer to give group totals as a percentage of report totals.*

7. Set the **Format** property to **Percent** from the drop down list.

8. Close the **Property Sheet** and switch to **Print Preview**.

9. The calculated percentage field shows that the 9 cats sold in this sale represent 6.87% of the total number of animals sold (if Driving Lesson 39 has not been completed, this value may be 25.00%).

10. Save and close the **Percentage Sold** report then close the database.

Driving Lesson 57 - Report Headers & Footers

▣ Park and Read

Reports can have header and footer areas defined. Group headers and footers are defined with grouping levels. Report headers and footers appear at the beginning and end of every report. Page headers and footers are printed at the top and bottom of every printed page. Data fields can be added to header and footer areas. These can include fields from the field list or the date and time. Automatic page numbering can be added to page headers or footers.

☞ Manoeuvres

1. Open the **Houses** database and the view the **Sample1** report.

2. Look at page 2. This page is still showing records from the first **Type of Property** group (**Apartment**), but because the field is defined in the Group Header it will not display until the start of the next group, i.e. there is no group heading on the second page.

3. Switch to **Design View**. Click and drag the **Type of Property** field straight upwards from the **Type of Property Header** to the **Page Header**, above the existing label.

4. View the report again. As the field is now in the **Page Header** it appears on every page.

5. Switch to **Design View**. Right click on the **Type of Property** field and select **Copy** from the shortcut menu.

6. Right click in the **Type of Property Footer** area and select **Paste**.

7. Delete the **Group Total** label (not the field) in this area and move the **Type of Property** field to take its place.

8. Paste the **Type of Property** field again, this time into the **Page Footer** area. Move it just to the right of the current date field.

                                                                      continued over

Driving Lesson 57 - Continued

9. View the report and look at page 2. The **Type of Property** field now appears in three places.

10. Switch to **Design View** and click on the **Type of Property** field in the **Page Footer**. Press <Delete> to remove it.

11. If a field was common throughout the whole report it could also be placed in **Report Header** or **Report Footer** in the same way. It is more common however to insert fields such as **Date**, **Time**, **Page Numbers** and **Labels** in these areas.

12. To insert the date, make sure the **Design** tab is displayed and click the **Date and Time** button in the **Header/Footer** group.

13. Select any date and time options and click **OK**. The fields are added to the right of the **Report Header** area.

14. To add page numbers, click the **Page Numbers** button from the **Header/Footer** group.

15. Select the **Format** option of **Page N of M**, the **Position** option of **Bottom of Page [Footer]**, and choose **Right** from the **Alignment** drop down list.

16. Click **OK**.

17. Use the **Label** tool, $\boxed{Aa}$, to draw a label in the centre of the **Page Footer**.

18. Type your name in the label.

19. Preview the report to see the information which has been added to the header and footer.

20. Leave the report open.

Driving Lesson 58 - Printing Reports

▣ Park and Read

It is possible to print out reports, either to show all pages, a selected page, or a range of pages.

↱ Manoeuvres

1. With the **Sample1** report open, click the **File** tab and select **Print** from the panel on the left. Three **Print** options are shown on the right.

2. Read of the descriptive text for each option then click **Print**. The **Print** dialog box is shown.

> **ℹ** *This dialog box is also available by clicking the **Print** button from the **Print Preview** tab.*

> **ℹ** *A range of pages or an individual page, can be printed using the **Pages** option and the number of copies can be specified at in the **Copies** area.*

3. Make sure the correct printer name is selected and **All** is selected from **Print Range**. Click **OK** to print the entire report.

4. Close the report without saving and close the database.

Driving Lesson 59 - Revision

This is not an ECDL test. Testing may only be carried out through certified ECDL test centres. This covers the features introduced in this section. Try not to refer to the preceding Driving Lessons while completing it.

1.   Open the **Supermarket** database.

2.   Use **Report Wizard** to create a report based on the **Stock** table.

3.   Show all available fields and group the report by **Category**.

4.   Include **Min** and **Max** summary values for **Price**.

5.   Use a **Stepped** layout, **Landscape** orientation.

6.   Name the report **Stock List**.

7.   In **Design View** create **Calculated Fields** to display the **Average Price** of the items in each category and for the whole report.

8.   Label the fields **Category Average** and **Report Average** respectively.

9.   Format all price fields as **Currency**.

10.   Print the report.

11.   Close the report and the database, saving any changes.

If you experienced any difficulty completing the Revision, refer back to the Driving Lessons in this section. Then redo the Revision.

Driving Lesson 60 - Revision

This covers the features introduced in this section. Try not to refer to the preceding Driving Lessons while completing it.

1. Use the **Country** database.

2. Create a query to find all of the countries with a population over 30 million. Save the query to use as the basis for a report in the next step.

[i] *Populations in this table are recorded in millions.*

3. Use the query above to produce a report displaying the following fields in the order specified: **Region**, **Country** and **Population**. Make the report stepped, grouped by **Region** and sorted in descending order of **Population**.

4. Give the report the title: **Highly Populated**.

5. Display the total and average population for each region. Insert the description **Total Population for this Region** alongside the total figure, and, insert the description **Average Population for this Region** alongside the average figure.

6. Change the **Format** properties of the total and average fields to **Fixed** with **0** decimal places (integers).

7. Add a calculated field to the detail (Country) record to show the population for that country as a percentage of the **Total Population** for that **Region**.

8. Print the report in portrait orientation with no page numbers and no date. Ensure all field headings and records are fully displayed.

9. Save and close the report.

10. Close the **Country** database.

If you experienced any difficulty completing the Revision, refer back to the Driving Lessons in this section. Then redo the Revision.

Once you are confident with the features, complete the Record of Achievement Matrix referring to the section at the end of the guide. Only when competent move on to the next Section.

Section 8
Import and Link
Data

By the end of this Section you should be able to:

Import Data from Spreadsheets

Import Data from Text Files

Import Data from Tables

Link a Database to External Data

To gain an understanding of the above features, work through the **Driving Lessons** in this **Section**.

For each **Driving Lesson**, read the **Park and Read** instructions, without touching the keyboard, then work through the numbered steps of the **Manoeuvres** on the computer. Complete the **Revision Exercise(s)** at the end of the section to test your knowledge.

Driving Lesson 61 - Importing Spreadsheets

▣ Park and Read

It is possible to **import** data from one database to another or from a different type of file such as spreadsheet or text file. This can be very useful if the data required for an *Access* application already exists in another location, either in a different database or in an *Excel* spreadsheet for example. Importing converts the source data format and creates a new copy of the data within *Access*. The data can be then edited in *Access,* and is completely independent of the source. This allows much greater flexibility for data entry.

⌒ Manoeuvres

1.   Open the **Contacts** database and select the **External Data** tab.

2.   Look in the **Import & Link** group and select the **Excel** button. A dialog box is displayed so that the source and destination of the imported file can be defined.

> ℹ *Notice there is an option to append the data to an existing table. This will add records to the end of the table, but great care must be taken so that the format of the imported data <u>exactly</u> matches the format of the existing table, or the import will fail.*

continued over

Driving Lesson 61 - Continued

3.   Use the **Browse** button to locate the folder with the supplied data files and select the file **Sick.xlsx**. Click **Open** to return to the dialog box.

4.   Select the option to import the data into a new table and click **OK**. The **Import Spreadsheet Wizard** appears.

5.   Specify that the **First Row Contains Column Headings**.

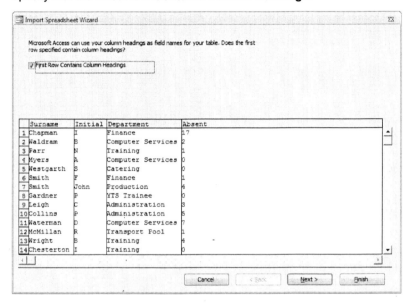

6.   Click **Next**. There are options here to change the names of any field or to choose to omit certain fields from the import process. Take no action but click **Next** again.

7.   There are options on this next screen to define one of the input fields as the **Primary Key** for the table or to allow *Access* to add a new field (a sequential number field) as the **Primary Key**. Select the third option, **No primary key** and click **Next**.

8.   Call the table **Sick List** and click **Finish** to create it. There is an option to save the import steps so they can be repeated easily but this will not be selected in this exercise. Click the **Close** button.

9.   A new table, **Sick List**, has been added to the database. Open the table to view the data and adjust the column widths if necessary.

10.   Save the table and close it but leave the database open.

Driving Lesson 62 - Importing Text Files

🅿 Park and Read

It is also possible to import text data into a database. The text file can be in any basic text format such as **.txt** (text) or **.csv** (comma separated variables).

Manoeuvres

1. With the **Contacts** database still open, select the **Text File** button, ▸ Text File from the **Import & Link** group on the **External Data** tab.

2. Browse to the supplied data folder, select the **tourists.csv** file and click **Open**. Select the option to import the data into a new table and click **OK**.

3. From the **Import Text Wizard** select **Delimited**.

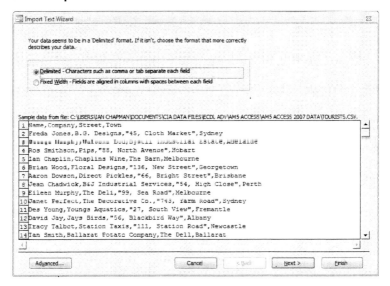

4. Click **Next** and select **Comma** as the **Delimiter**. Select quotes (") as the **Text Qualifier** (all text within quotes will then be treated as a single field).

continued over

Driving Lesson 62 - Continued

 *The data in the source file must be divided into individual fields by a delimiter of some form. The Delimiter character will vary depending on the type of text file being imported. It is **Comma** for **.csv** files, and is often **Tab** for a table in a **.txt** file. Check the source file if necessary to establish the delimiter.*

5.   Check **First Row Contains Field Names** and click Next and **Next** again.

6.   Choose **No primary key** and click **Next**.

7.   Call the table **Tourist List** and click **Finish**. Click **Close** when the **Save Import Steps** prompt is shown.

8.   View the new table, adjust the column widths where necessary, then save and close it.

9.   Following the steps above, import the text file **Colleagues.txt** into a new table called **Holiday List**. It is separated by **Tab Delimiter**.

 *Files in various formats, e.g. Paradox and dBASE can be imported into an Access database. XML files can also be imported - this is a type of language particularly suited to the Internet and helps information systems share structural data. Select the correct **File Type** from the **Import** dialog box and follow the **Import Wizard** steps.*

10.   Leave the database open for the next Driving Lesson.

Driving Lesson 63 - Importing Tables

▣ Park and Read

Importing data from a table in another database is very simple as the data is already in the correct format.

⌐ Manoeuvres

1. With the **Contacts** database still open, display the **External Data** tab and click the **Access** button from the **Import & Link** group.

2. Use the **Browse** button to locate the folder with the supplied data files and select the **CiA** database. Click **Open** to return to the dialog box.

3. Select the option to **Import tables**, etc. and click **OK**. The **Import Objects** dialog box appears. Select the **Tables** tab in the dialog box.

 *Any object can be imported, but there is no point importing a **Form** or a **Report** for example, unless the matching tables were present.*

4. Select the **Suppliers** table and click **OK**. Click **Close** in the **Save Import Steps** prompt. The table is imported into the **Contacts** database.

5. Open the **Suppliers** table in **Design View** then **Datasheet View**. All formatting and data has been copied.

⚹ *This is a separate copy of the table, completely independent of the original.*

6. Close the table and the database.

Driving Lesson 64 - Linking Data

🅿 Park and Read

Linking involves creating a database table from an external source such as a spreadsheet or a table in another database, without creating a separate copy of the object source within the database.

Any changes to the source are automatically reflected in the linked table. Content cannot be changed directly in tables linked to spreadsheets, although it can be in tables linked to other tables. Design changes <u>cannot</u> be made directly to any linked table in a database.

A disadvantage is that if the source file is ever moved or deleted, the database table will no longer be available.

Manoeuvres

1. Open the **CiA** database and select the **External Data** tab.

2. Look in the **Import & Link** group and select the **Excel** button. A dialog box is displayed so that the source and destination of the imported file can be defined.

3. Use the **Browse** button to locate the file **Sick.xlsx** in the supplied data.

> ℹ️ *To link to text files (.**txt**), or comma separated variable files (.**csv**), select the* ***Text File*** *button and browse for the appropriate file.*

4. Set the following option in the dialog box.

   > ◉ **Link to the data source by creating a linked table.**
   > Access will create a table that will maintain a link to the source data in Excel. Changes made to the source data in Excel will be reflected in the linked table. However, the source data cannot be changed from within Access.

5. Click **OK**. When the **Link Spreadsheet Wizard** is displayed check the **First Row Contains Column Headings** box and click **Next**.

6. Name the table **Sick List Linked** and click **Finish**. Click **OK** at the prompt. The new table is shown in the **Navigation Pane**.

continued over

Driving Lesson 64 - Continued

7. The new icon indicates that the new table is linked to information from *Excel*. Double click on the icon to open the table.

8. Try to change the number of days' absence for **I Chapman**. This is not allowed. Content can only be changed in the source.

9. Switch to **Design View** for the table. There will be a warning that design changes are not possible.

10. Click **No** then close the table.

11. Open *Excel* and the **Sick** workbook. Change the number of days' absence for **I Chapman** to **34**, save the workbook and close *Excel*.

12. Open the **Sick List** Linked table from the CiA database to see the changes made in Excel have been applied here.

13. Close the table and use *Windows Explorer* or some other means, to rename **Sick.xlsx** as **Sickcopy.xlsx**.

14. Try to open the **Sick List Linked** table from the **CiA** database again. This will not be allowed now because *Access* can no longer find the source file **Sick.xlsx**. Click **OK** at the error message.

15. To link to a database table, display the **External Data** tab and click the **Access** button.

16. Use **Browse** to select the **Staff** database from the supplied data and click **Open**.

17. Select the **Link to** option and click **OK**.

18. Select the **Staff List** table and click **OK**. Staff List is added to the database as a Linked Table.

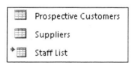

19. Open the table in **Datasheet View**. The link is now 'two way'. Data changes can be made here and will be applied to the original table. Design changes are still restricted.

20. Close the table and the database.

21. Rename **Sickcopy** back to **Sick**.

22. Leave *Access* open but close all other open applications.

Driving Lesson 65 - Revision

This is not an ECDL test. Testing may only be carried out through certified ECDL test centres. This covers the features introduced in this section. Try not to refer to the preceding Driving Lessons while completing it.

1.   Create a new database called **Awards**.

2.   Import data from the *Microsoft Excel* file **Oscar**.

3.   On the first Wizard screen click the option for **First Row Contains Column Headings**. There is a message that some of the column headings cannot be used as *Access* field names. Click **OK** to continue.

4.   Create a new table for the data and accept all fields.

5.   Choose the **Year** field as your own primary key and name the table **Oscar**.

6.   Examine the **Oscar** table in *Access* and widen the columns if necessary to see the headings clearly. Look at the field names in the column headings. Some of them were supplied by *Access* rather than taken from the spreadsheet. By examining the original **Oscar** spreadsheet file in *Excel*, explain why the original column headings could not be used.

7.   Close the table and the database, saving any changes.

8.   Close *Excel*.

$\boxed{\mathbf{i}}$ *Answers are shown in the **Answers** section at the end of this guide.*

If you experienced any difficulty completing the Revision, refer back to the Driving Lessons in this section. Then redo the Revision.

Driving Lesson 66 - Revision

This covers the features introduced in this section. Try not to refer to the preceding Driving Lessons while completing it.

1. Open the **Custom Computers** database.

2. Import the **Staff List** table from the **Personnel** database as a **Linked** table.

3. In the **Custom Computers** database create a new summary query based on data from the linked **Staff List** table to sum the salaries for all staff. Make a note of the total value.

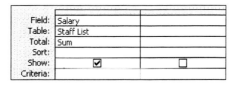

4. Save the query as **Salary** and close it.

5. Open the **Personnel** database and the **Staff List** table.

6. Change the salary for the first record (**Peter Nyder**) to £28,000.

7. Close the table and the database.

8. Open the **Custom Computers** database and run the **Salary** query. What is the new total?

9. Close the query and database.

*Answers are shown in the **Answers** section at the end of this guide.*

If you experienced any difficulty completing the Revision, refer back to the Driving Lessons in this section. Then redo the Revision.

Once you are confident with the features, complete the Record of Achievement Matrix referring to the section at the end of the guide. Only when competent move on to the next Section.

Section 9
Action Queries

By the end of this Section you should be able to:

Create Append Queries

Create Delete Queries

Make a Table from a Query

Create an Update Query

To gain an understanding of the above features, work through the **Driving Lessons** in this **Section**.

For each **Driving Lesson**, read the **Park and Read** instructions, without touching the keyboard, then work through the numbered steps of the **Manoeuvres** on the computer. Complete the **Revision Exercise(s)** at the end of the section to test your knowledge.

Driving Lesson 67 - Append Query

▣ Park and Read

An **Append Query** selects a group of records from one table using all the features of a query, and adds them to the end of another table. Note that the information is not removed from the original table.

⌒ Manoeuvres

1. Open the **CiA** database.

2. Some **Action** queries are controlled by security settings in *Access*. If there is a **Security Warning** displayed under the **Ribbon**, click **Enable Content**.

ⓘ *Depending on your security settings, you may have to select **Enable** from a list of options and click **OK**.*

3. Select the **Create** tab and click on **Query Design** to start a new query. This query is to search the **Prospective Customers** table and select those records with a status of **A** (this has been entered to mark **Prospective** customers who have now become **Actual** customers). These records will be automatically added to the **Customer Details** table.

4. From the **Show Table** dialog box choose the **Prospective Customers** table. Click **Add** and **Close**.

5. Make sure the **Design** tab is displayed and click the **Append** query button from the **Query Type** area.

6. The **Append** dialog box appears. From **Table Name** select **Customer Details** as the table to which the records are to be added.

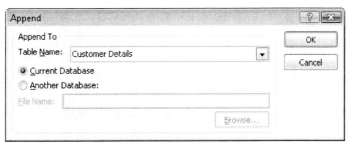

7. Click **OK**. A new row appears on the query grid, **Append To**:

8. Place the **Customer Ref** field on to the grid. Notice **Append To** also contains **Customer Ref**. This is the name of the field as it will appear in the **Customer Details** table.

continued over

Driving Lesson 67 - Continued

9. Place the following fields on to the grid: **Title, First Name, Surname, Company, Address, County, Telephone, Fax, Information** and **Status**.

10. Each field on the grid, except **County** and **Status**, has an **Append To** value, indicating the field on the new table that will be updated.

11. The **County** field has a different name in the **Customer Details** table. Enter **Town** in **Append To** for this field. The **Town** field in the **Customer Details** table will be updated by the content in **County** from **Prospective Customers**.

12. The **Status** field has no **Append To** value because there is no matching field on the **Customer Details** table. Leaving the **Append To** value blank means that this field will not be included in the append process.

13. The field is however used in the selection process. Under **Status** enter **A**, in **Criteria**. Only records with this status are to be selected.

14. To view the information that is to be appended without actually appending it, click on the **Datasheet** button ⊞, prior to **Run**. This will show the records that will be appended.

15. Return to the **Query Design** and click **Run**, [Run].

16. A dialog box appears stating how many records will be appended.

17. Click **Yes** to append the records to the target table.

ℹ️ *Records which are appended are not deleted from the source table. The 5 records added here still exist on the **Prospective Customers** table.*

18. Save the query as **Append New Customers**. The query can now be run whenever required and will take any records flagged as new customers and add them to the **Customer Details** table.

19. Close the query and open up the **Customer Details** table to view the appended records (the first 5).

20. Close the table but leave the database open for the next Driving Lesson.

Driving Lesson 68 - Delete Query

Park and Read

A **Delete Query** will delete a selected group of records from one or more tables. This could be run after an **Append** query for example, to remove all the updated records from the original table.

Manoeuvres

1. With the **CiA** database still open, start a new query in **Design View**. Add the **Prospective Customers** table to the query grid and close the **Show Table** dialog box.

2. Choose the **Delete** option, from the **Query Type** area of the **Design** tab.

3. Add **Customer Ref, Company** and **Status** to the grid and specify the **Criteria** as **A**, in the **Status** field.

Field:	Customer Ref	Company	Status
Table:	Prospective Customer	Prospective Customer	Prospective Customer
Delete:	Where	Where	Where
Criteria:			"A"
or:			

4. Click the **Datasheet** button to view the records that will be deleted. These are the same records that were appended to the **Customer Details** table.

Any number of fields can be added to the grid to view exactly which records are selected, but it is the <u>whole</u> record that will always be deleted.

5. Return to **Design View** and **Run** the query,

6. Click **Yes** to confirm the deletion, then save the query as **Delete Appended Records** and close it.

7. Open the **Prospective Customers** table. All the customers whose **Status** was **A** should now be deleted.

8. Close the table but leave the database open for the next Driving Lesson.

Driving Lesson 69 - Make-Table Query

🅿 Park and Read

A **Make-Table Query** selects data from one or more tables, using all the features of a query, and creates a new table from that data. Not all the fields from the original table(s) need to be included in the new table.

↱ Manoeuvres

1.   A table is to be made containing all the unpaid orders. From the **CiA** database start a new query in **Design View** and add the **Customer Details** and **Orders** tables to the query grid.

2.   Choose the **Make Table** query option, from the **Query Type** area of the **Design** tab.

3.   At the dialog box enter the **Table Name** as **Unpaid Orders**.

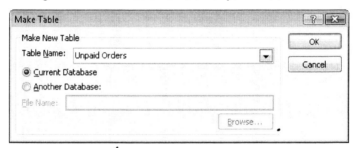

4.   Click **OK**. From **Customer Details** place the **Title**, **First Name**, **Surname**, **Company** and **Telephone** fields on to the grid. From **Orders**, place the **Order Ref**, **Order Date** and **Paid** fields on to the grid.

5.   Specify the **Criteria** for **Paid** as **No**. **Uncheck** the **Show** box for **Paid**, this means that this field will not be included in the new records.

6.   **Run** the query. Select **Yes** at the dialog box.

7.   Save the query and name it **Make Unpaid Orders Table**. Close it.

continued over

Driving Lesson 69 - Continued

8.   Open the **Unpaid Orders** table to view the data. A table has been created to hold details of all orders which are currently unpaid.

9.   Close the table and open the **Make Unpaid Orders Table** query in **Design View**.

10. The query is to be modified. Delete the **First Name** from the query grid.

11. Save and run the query.

12. There is a prompt that the existing table will be deleted. Click **Yes** and then **Yes** again at the next prompt. A new table is created, replacing the original.

13. Close the query.

14. View the **Unpaid Orders** table. Notice that the **First Name** field has been removed.

15. Close the table but leave the database open.

Driving Lesson 70 - Update Query

Park and Read

An **Update Query** will update a specific field within a table(s). For example, increasing all prices by 10%, changing a name of a product, etc.

Manoeuvres

1. From the **CiA** database, open the **Products** table and note the prices of the first 5 items.

2. Close the table and start a new query in **Design View** based on the **Products** table. From the **Query Type** area on the **Design** tab select **Update**.

3. Place the **Price** field on to the grid. In **Update To:** enter **[Price]*1.1** and in **Criteria** enter **>=10**. This will update prices of all **Products** which cost **£10** or more, by **10%**.

Field:	Price
Table:	Products
Update To:	[Price]*1.1
Criteria:	>=10
or:	

4. Click the **Datasheet** button to view the data that will be updated.

5. Return to **Design View** and **Run** the query.

Microsoft Access

You are about to update 13 row(s).

Once you click Yes, you can't use the Undo command to reverse the changes. Are you sure you want to update these records?

Yes   No

6. Click **Yes** at the update prompt, save the query as **Update Prices** and close it.

7. Open the **Products** table again and view the updated prices for the first five records. All prices for products that used to cost £10 or more are now increased by **10%**.

8. Close the table and view the query in **Design View**. There's been a management decision to increase prices by a further 5%.

9. Change the calculation to **[Price]*1.05** and run the query, clicking **Yes** at the prompt.

10. Save and close the query and open the **Products** table to check the modified prices.

11. Close the database.

*Answers are shown in the **Answers** section at the end of this guide.*

Driving Lesson 71 - Revision

This is not an ECDL test. Testing may only be carried out through certified ECDL test centres. This covers the features introduced in this section. Try not to refer to the preceding Driving Lessons while completing it.

1. Open the **Transport** database. If there is a **Security Warning** displayed under the **Ribbon**, select **Enable Content** and click **OK**.

2. Create a **Make Table** query containing all the fields from the **Buses** table.

3. Set the criteria to only pick out Buses whose number of **Journeys** is **4**. Call the query **4journeys** and the table **Top Routes**.

4. Using an **Append** query, add all the records from the **Buses** table whose number of **Journeys** is **3,** to the **Top Routes** table. Call the query **3journeys**.

5. Create a query to delete any bus from the **Top Routes** table whose **Size** is **Mini**, calling the query **Delete Minis**.

6. Create an **Update** query called **Change Name** to change all **Size** values of **Single** to **Coach** in the **Top Routes** table.

7. Close all the objects and the database.

If you experienced any difficulty completing the Revision, refer back to the Driving Lessons in this section. Then redo the Revision.

Driving Lesson 72 - Revision

This covers the features introduced in this section. Try not to refer to the preceding Driving Lessons while completing it.

1. Open the **Sales** database and select **Enable Content** if prompted. Bill Anderson has retired. His position as Northern area manager is to be filled by Phil Smith.

2. Create an **Update Query** based on the **Sales Figures** table to make the change.

3. Place the **Area** and **Manager** fields on to the grid.

4. For the **Area Criteria**, enter **Northern**.

5. For **Update To** in the **Manager** field, enter **Phil Smith**.

6. Save the query as **Northern Replacement**.

7. Run the query and view the changes to the **Sales Figures** table.

8. Use a **Make Table Query** to create a new table containing any sales above **£15,000**.

9. Name the new table **Top Ten**.

10. Select the **Sales Figures** table and add the **Last Name**, **Area** and **Sales** fields to the grid.

11. For the **Sales Criteria**, enter **>15000** and save the query as **Top Sales**.

12. Run the query, then close it.

13. Open the **Top Ten** table.

14. Which area includes the highest sales value?

15. Who is the salesperson with the highest sales for the **Eastern** region?

16. Close the table and the database.

i   *Answers are shown in the **Answers** section at the end of this guide.*

If you experienced any difficulty completing the Revision, refer back to the Driving Lessons in this section. Then redo the Revision.

Once you are confident with the features, complete the Record of Achievement Matrix referring to the section at the end of the guide. Only when competent move on to the next Section.

Section 10
Query Wizards

By the end of this Section you should be able to:

Create a Crosstab Query

Create a Find Duplicates Query

Create a Find Unmatched Query

To gain an understanding of the above features, work through the **Driving Lessons** in this **Section**.

For each **Driving Lesson**, read the **Park and Read** instructions, without touching the keyboard, then work through the numbered steps of the **Manoeuvres** on the computer. Complete the **Revision Exercise(s)** at the end of the section to test your knowledge.

Driving Lesson 73 - Crosstab Query

🅿 Park and Read

By default, a line on a query result represents a record of some kind. A **Crosstab Query** however shows summarised values such as **Sum**, **Avg**, **Count**, **Max**, **Min**, etc. for fields within a table or query and groups them together into a matrix type of display. The columns and rows of the matrix can be any fields from the table or query. Crosstab queries can either be created via the wizard or manually. It is recommended to use the wizard.

⌐ Manoeuvres

1. Open the **CiA** database and create a query to include the following tables and fields.

Customer Details	Orders	Order Details	Products
Company		Amount	Product

 *Even though there are no fields used from the **Orders** table, it needs to be included in the query to maintain the relationships between all the other tables.*

2. Save the query as **Product Info** and close it.

3. From the **Create** tab select **Query Wizard** and select **Crosstab Query Wizard** from the dialog box. Click **OK**.

4. Choose the **Queries** option from **View**, then select **Product Info** as the source of the data for this crosstab query.

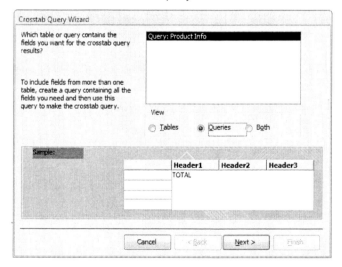

continued over

Driving Lesson 73 - Continued

5.   Click **Next**. Click on **Company** then [>] to select that field for the **row headings**.

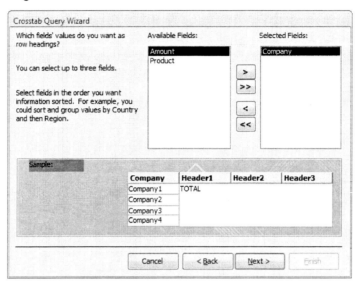

6.   Notice that the lower half of each wizard screen shows a sample of the final query, as far as it has been defined. Click **Next** then select **Product** to specify that for the **column headings**.

Company	Product1	Product2	Product3
Company1	TOTAL		
Company2			
Company3			
Company4			

7.   Click **Next**. Select the **Amount** field, then the **Sum** function.

8.   Click **Next**.

Company	Product1	Product2	Product3
Company1	Sum(Amount)		
Company2			
Company3			
Company4			

9.   Name the query **Product Info Results**.

10. Click **Finish** to view the results. The query is a grid of the total amount of products each company has bought.

11. To modify the query, switch to **Design View**, click in the **Sort** field for **Company**, and select **Ascending**.

12. Save and run the query.

13. Notice how the results are now sorted alphabetically by **Company**.

14. Close the query but leave the database open.

Driving Lesson 74 - Find Duplicates Query

▣ Park and Read

A **Find Duplicates Query** will search a table for records where individual fields have duplicate values. For example, company details that may have been entered twice by mistake.

℞ Manoeuvres

1. A query is to be created to find companies who appear more than once in the database. From the **CiA** database click **Query Wizard** from the **Create** tab and select **Find Duplicates Query Wizard** from the dialog box. Click **OK**.

2. Choose the **Customer Details** table and click **Next**.

3. Select **Company** and click ⌊ > ⌋, then select **Address** and click ⌊ > ⌋.

4. By selecting two fields here, both fields must match before records will be selected as duplicates. In this example, two records with the same **Company** name but different **Address** fields will <u>not</u> be selected as duplicates. Click **Next**.

5. Click ⌊ >> ⌋ to show all the fields in the query results then click **Next**.

6. Finally, name the query **Duplicate Company Details**.

7. Click **Finish**. The results contain the details of the companies that appear more than once with the same address in the **Customer Details** table.

8. On the **Home** tab, switch to **Design View** and remove the **Fax** field from the query grid.

9. Save the query and view the changes.

10. Close the query but leave the database open.

Driving Lesson 75 - Find Unmatched Query

▣ Park and Read

The **Find Unmatched Query** finds records in one table that do not have a matching record in another table. For example, **Customers** who do not have records on an **Orders** table or **Students** with no records on a **Courses** table.

⌕ Manoeuvres

1. A query is to be created to find all the companies who have not made any orders. In the **CiA** database click **Query Wizard** from the **Create** tab.

2. Select **Find Unmatched Query Wizard** from the dialog box. Click **OK**.

3. Select the **Customer Details** table as the table that contains the information. Click **Next**.

4. Select **Orders** as the table that has the related information to be searched. Click **Next**.

5. Highlight the **Customer Ref** in both tables and click <kbd><=></kbd>.

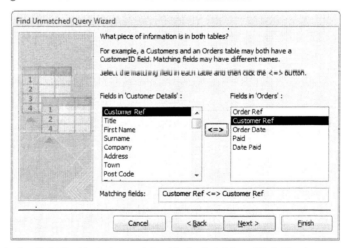

6. This is the field that is to be matched in both tables. Click **Next**.

7. Click <kbd>>></kbd>, to view all the fields in the query results. Click **Next**.

8. Name the query **No Orders**. Click **Finish** to view the results. A list of all the customers who have not placed any orders appears.

ℹ *To modify a **Find Unmatched** query, make the changes in **Design View**. If major changes are required, it may be better to create a new query.*

9. Close the query and the database.

Driving Lesson 76 - Revision

This is not an ECDL test. Testing may only be carried out through certified ECDL test centres. This covers the features introduced in this section. Try not to refer to the preceding Driving Lessons while completing it.

1.   Open the **Premises** database.

2.   Use the wizard to create a query which will display all the properties which have exactly the same price as another property on the **Commercial** table.

3.   As well as **Price**, show the fields **Property Ref**, **Location** and **Address**.

4.   Call the query **Same Price**.

5.   Close the query.

6.   Use the wizard to create a **Crosstab** query which show the total number of each **Type** of premises in each **Location**.

7.   Name it **Properties**.

8.   Close the query and the database.

If you experienced any difficulty completing the Revision, refer back to the Driving Lessons in this section. Then redo the Revision.

Once you are confident with the features, complete the Record of Achievement Matrix referring to the section at the end of the guide. Only when competent move on to the next Section.

Section 11
Macros

By the end of this Section you should be able to:

Understand Macro Actions

Create a Macro

Attach a Macro to a Control or Object

Create Macros from Controls

Create Command Button Macros

To gain an understanding of the above features, work through the **Driving Lessons** in this **Section**.

For each **Driving Lesson**, read the **Park and Read** instructions, without touching the keyboard, then work through the numbered steps of the **Manoeuvres** on the computer. Complete the **Revision Exercise(s)** at the end of the section to test your knowledge.

Driving Lesson 77 - Create a New Macro

Park and Read

Macros are easily created and this usually involves selecting **Actions** and specifying **Action Arguments** to control the operation of each action. For example, an **Open Form** macro can be created to open a specified form. **Action Arguments** must be set up to state which form is to be opened and if the form is to be viewed in **Form**, **Design** or **Datasheet View**. Other **Action Arguments** can be used to set controls for the form, such as whether data can be added, edited or whether the form is to be read-only.

Note that the commands **Minimize** and **Maximize** which are used in this exercise have no visible effect in **Tabbed Documents** mode. If it wished to see these effects in operation, open the database in **Overlapping Windows** mode and run the macros again.

Manoeuvres

1. Open the **Transport** database.

2. Some macros are controlled by security settings in *Access*. If there is a **Security Warning** displayed under the **Ribbon**, click **Enable Content**. Do this when opening databases for all exercises in this section.

3. Display the **Create** tab and select the **Macro** button to create a new macro. The **Macro** window appears.

4. Click the drop down arrow in the empty **Action** box to display a list of available actions.

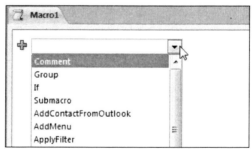

5. Scroll down the list and select **OpenForm**. An expanded **Action** box is displayed for the **OpenForm** action, containing all the arguments that apply for this particular action.

Actions can also be added by locating and double clicking the required action in the **Action Catalog** panel on the right of the window. If this panel is not shown, click the **Action Catalog** from the **Macro Tools Design** tab.

continued over

Driving Lesson 77 - Continued

6. Click the drop down arrow in **Form Name** and choose the name of the form that is to be opened – **Servicing**. Leave the **View** argument as **Form**. This defines the view that will be used when the form is opened.

7. In the new **Action** box positioned below the **OpenForm** action, select **MinimizeWindow** as an action on the line. This is a simple function to minimise the display and has no **Arguments**.

8. Click Collapse All on the Macro Tools Design tab

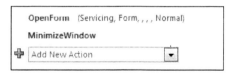

9. Save the macro and name it **OpenServicing**.

10. Click **OK** and close the **Macro** window.

11. From the **Database Window**, double click the **OpenServicing** macro. The **Servicing** form opens and the **Minimize** command is run.

i *Minimize and Maximize will only have a visible effect for objects displayed in Overlapping Windows mode.*

12. Close the form.

13. Open the **OpenServicing** macro in **Design View**. Select the **MinimizeWindow** action and press <**Delete**>. Add a new action of **MaximizeWindow**. Next time the macro is used the form will be opened and maximised.

14. Save the macro and close it, but leave the database open.

Driving Lesson 78 - Attaching a Macro to a Control

◨ Park and Read

Once a macro has been created, it can be attached to various controls on a form, such as a data field, image or command button. It can also be attached to the whole form.

When it has been attached, an **Event** needs to be set up in the properties of the control. This defines what will cause the macro to run, e.g. on a single or double click of the mouse, or when the field is updated, or the when the form is opened. The possible events will vary with the type of control.

⌒ Manoeuvres

1. In the **Transport** database, create a new macro. The first action is **CloseWindow**. By default it will close the current window. Set the **Save** argument to **No**.

2. The second action is **OpenForm**, with a **Form Name** of **Servicing**. Select the **Collapse All** button.

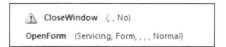

⚠ CloseWindow (, No)

OpenForm (Servicing, Form, , , , Normal)

3. Save the macro as **Testmacro** and close it.

4. Create another new macro and select **Show All Actions** from the **Design** tab to make more macro actions available in the list.

Show All Actions

5. Make the first action **PrintOut** with the arguments as shown below.

⊟ ⚠ PrintOut		×
Print Range	Selection	▾
Page From		
Page To		
Print Quality	Medium	▾
Copies	1.0	
Collate Copies	Yes	▾

ℹ *The **Selection** argument means that only the selected record will be printed.*

6. Add a second action of **CloseWindow**.

7. Set the **Save** argument for the **CloseWindow** action to **No**. Save the macro as **Printmacro** and close it.

continued over

Driving Lesson 78 - Continued

8. Open the **Buses** form in **Design View**. Ensure that the **Use Control Wizards** button is turned <u>off</u>.

9. Create a **Command Button** at the left of the **Form Footer**.

10. With the **Command Button** selected, view its **Property Sheet**.

11. Select the **Event** tab and click in **On Click** from the property list, i.e. a single click on this button will run the macro.

12. To select which macro to run click the down arrow - a list of available macros is shown.

13. Choose the **Testmacro** macro.

14. Select the **Format** tab and in **Caption**, enter **Service**. This will appear on the button.

15. Macros can be attached to other controls on the form. Click on the image in the centre of the page and view its **Property Sheet**. Select the **Event** tab.

16. Click in **On Dbl Click** from the property list, i.e. a double click on this object will be needed to run the macro.

17. Click the down arrow and choose the **Printmacro** macro.

18. Click in the **Size** field and view its **Property Sheet**. Select the **Event** tab.

19. Click in **On Key Press** from the property list, i.e. any key press in this field will run the macro.

20. Click the down arrow and choose the **Testmacro** macro.

21. Close the **Property Sheet**. Save the form.

22. Switch to **Form View** and click the **Service** button on the form. The **Testmacro** macro runs. The form is closed and the **Servicing** form opens.

23. Close the **Servicing** form and open the **Buses** form again in **Form View**.

24. Move to record 3 and double click the central image. The macro **Printmacro** runs. The record is printed and the form closes.

25. Open the **Buses** form again and click in the **Size** field.

26. Press any character key on the keyboard. The **Testmacro** macro runs. The form is closed and the **Servicing** form opens.

27. Close the **Servicing** form and leave the **Transport** database open.

Driving Lesson 79 - Attaching a Macro to an Object

▣ Park and Read

Macros can also be assigned to a database object such as a whole form.

ℝ Manoeuvres

1. In the **Transport** database, open the **Buses** form in **Design View**.

2. Click on the button in the top left to select the whole form.

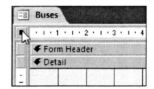

3. Display the **Property Sheet** and select the **Event** tab. Notice there are many more possible events associated with the whole form.

4. Click in **On Close** from the property list, i.e. the macro will be triggered when the form is closed.

5. Click the down arrow and choose the **OpenServicing** macro.

6. Close the **Property Sheet**. Save the form.

7. Switch to **Form View**. Navigate through a few records and then close the form. The **OpenServicing** macro runs and the **Servicing** form opens in maximised format.

8. Close the **Servicing** form and display the **Buses** form in **Design View**.

9. Remove the **OpenServicing** macro from the **On Close** event for the form.

10. Save and close the **Buses** form but leave the database open.

Driving Lesson 80 - Create Macros from Controls

▣ Park and Read

Instead of creating the macro then attaching it to a control, it is possible to create the macro as the control itself is being added to the form (or report). As before, the control can be a button, a field or the form itself. The created macro is embedded with the form.

The **Find** macro, which is created here, uses the **Find and Replace** function to search for records using the field specified in the **Action Argument** for the command.

⌒ Manoeuvres

1. From the **Transport** database, open the **Buses** form in **Design View**.

2. Ensure the **Use Control Wizards** option is turned off. Create a **Command Button** at the right of the **Form Footer** and view the **Property Sheet**.

3. Select the **Event** tab and select **On Click**, i.e. the event will be triggered when the button is clicked.

4. Instead of selecting an existing macro, click on the **Build** button, ⌐┅┘. The **Choose Builder** dialog box appears. Select **Macro Builder** and click **OK**.

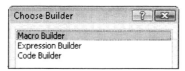

5. The **Macro Window** appears. Select the **GoToControl Action** and in the **Action Arguments**, enter **Fleet Number** as the **Control Name**, because this is the field that will be used during the **Find and Replace** process.

6. On the next **Action** line, choose the **RunMenuCommand Action** and from the **Action Arguments** click in **Command** and select **Find**. This will run the **Find and Replace** command.

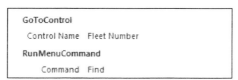

continued over

Driving Lesson 80 - Continued

7.   Close the **Macro** window. A prompt will appear.

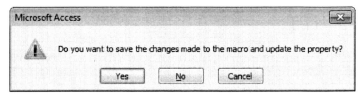

8.   Select **Yes** and the macro will be stored as an embedded object within the form definition. This is shown in the **Property Sheet**.

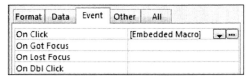

9.   On the **Format** tab, change the **Caption** to **Find**. This will appear on the command button.

10. Close the **Property Sheet**, save the form and switch to **Form View**.

11. Click the **Find** button. The **Find and Replace** dialog box appears. Enter the fleet number **L12** in **Find What**.

12. Click **Find Next**. The first matching record appears. What is the driver's first name? Move the dialog box if necessary to see the form.

i   *Answers are shown in the **Answers** section at the end of this guide.*

13. Close the **Find** dialog box.

14. Close the form and leave the database open.

Driving Lesson 81 - Command Button Macros

▣ Park and Read

Macros can be added easily when creating command buttons using the wizard.

⌐ Manoeuvres

1. From the **Transport** database, open the **Buses** form in **Design View**.

2. Make sure **Use Control Wizards** is switched on, then create a command button in the centre of the **Form Footer**.

3. Select **Miscellaneous** from the list of **Categories** list and **Run Macro** from the list of **Actions**.

ℹ️ *There are options here to attach operations without directly creating a macro.*

4. Click **Next**. Select **Printmacro** from the list and click **Next** again.

5. Select **Text** and type **Print Record** as the text to appear on the button.

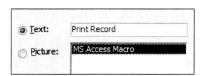

6. Click **Next**. Leave the name unchanged and click **Finish**.

7. Save the form and switch to **Form View**.

8. Click the **Print Record** button to print out a copy of the current record.

9. Close the **Transport** database.

Driving Lesson 82 - Revision

This is not an ECDL test. Testing may only be carried out through certified ECDL test centres. This covers the features introduced in this section. Try not to refer to the preceding Driving Lessons while completing it.

1.   Open the **Staff** database.

2.   Create a macro to open the **Staff List** table (use the **OpenTable** action) in **Datasheet View**.

3.   Add a second action to **Maximize** the display.

4.   Save the macro as **ShowStaff** and close it.

5.   Create another macro to print the currently selected record and then to close the form.

6.   Save the macro as **Printrecord** and close it.

7.   Open the **Staff Info** form in **Design View** and select the **Employee No** control. Attach the **Show Staff** macro to this control so that it is activated when the control is double clicked.

8.   Create a **Command Button** in the lower part of the **Detail** area. Attach the macro **Printrecord** to the button. Change the button caption to **Print this Record**.

9.   Save the form, switch to **Form View** and double click in **Employee No**.

10. Close the **Staff List** table when it opens.

11. Click the **Print this Record** button to print the record and close the form.

12. Close the database.

If you experienced any difficulty completing the Revision, refer back to the Driving Lessons in this section. Then redo the Revision.

Driving Lesson 83 - Revision

This covers the features introduced in this section. Try not to refer to the preceding Driving Lessons while completing it.

1. Open the database **Supermarket** and the **Delete Stock** form in **Design View**.

2. Create a command button in the form footer.

3. View the properties for the button and on the **Format** tab, change the **Caption** to **Delete Record**.

4. Select the **Event** tab and the **On Click** property and then click the **Build** button.

5. Choose the **Macro Builder**.

6. Set the first **Action** as **MessageBox** and the **Message** as **Are you sure you want to delete this record?**

7. Make sure **Beep** is set to **Yes**.

8. From **Type**, select **Warning?**

9. In **Title**, enter **Delete Record**.

10. For the next **Action**, select **RunMenuCommand** and in **Command** choose **DeleteRecord`**.

11. Save the macro as **DeleteRecord**.

12. Close the macro, saving if prompted.

13. Switch to **Form View** and move to record **15**.

14. Test the button. Click **OK** when the **Delete Record** message appears and click **Yes** at the next prompt.

15. Close the form and the database, saving any changes.

If you experienced any difficulty completing the Revision, refer back to the Driving Lessons in this section. Then redo the Revision.

Answers

Driving Lesson 6

Step 7   Data is retrieved from 4 tables.

Driving Lesson 16

Step 7   £57,285.71

Step 9   £104,525.00

Driving Lesson 17

Step 3

Location	MaxOfPrice	MinOfPrice
Central Area	£300,000.00	£56,000.00
Dockland	£120,000.00	£38,000.00
Enterprise Centre	£200,000.00	£45,000.00
Industrial Park	£176,000.00	£34,000.00
Riverside Complex	£250,000.00	£43,000.00
Valley Grove	£150,000.00	£44,000.00

Step 7

Location	Price	Address
Industrial Park	£34,000.00	Unit 2 Boreham Close
Dockland	£38,000.00	17 The Port Buildings
Riverside Complex	£43,000.00	6 Shore Road
Valley Grove	£44,000.00	Unit 68
Enterprise Centre	£45,000.00	17 Cider Place

Step 9

Location	Price	Address
Central Area	£300,000.00	Raby Exhibition Hall
Riverside Complex	£250,000.00	Jupiter Suite
Central Area	£250,000.00	5th Floor, Stanton Tower
Enterprise Centre	£200,000.00	Unit D, Main Building
Central Area	£200,000.00	15 Lothian Enterprise Building
Industrial Park	£176,000.00	7 Elm Court
Enterprise Centre	£175,000.00	86 Kingsway
Central Area	£156,000.00	17 Hartson Chambers
Valley Grove	£150,000.00	12 Desert Road
Riverside Complex	£150,000.00	Suite A, The Marina

Driving Lesson 21

Step 2   There are 6 different engineers.

Step 3   Minimum price £26, maximum price £390.

Step 4   Total price £2550.

Step 5   Keith (£243.00)

Step 8   Keith has 3 jobs over £100.

Step 12   **Like "?#5".** 6 records are found.

Driving Lesson 22

Step 3   Apartment.

Step 7   32a Stanton Tower.

Step 9   8 Sunset Avenue.

Driving Lesson 31

Step 6 3.

Step 7 Because there are records for **JT** on the **Meetings** table and **Cascade** has not been specified.

Step 9 Yes, the **Meetings** table is automatically updated.

Step 10 Because there is no related record with a key of **AS** on **People**.

Driving Lesson 32

Step 6

First Name	Personal records.Surname	Personally referred by
▶ Harry	Hill	Ball
Beryl	Barrington	Ball
Cheryl	Cannock	Barrington
*		

Step 11 4 introductions.

Step 13 10 records

Driving Lesson 37

Step 8 Sandstone Computers shows one record per computer, with repairs shown in a subform. Multitable shows one record for each computer/repair combination.

Driving Lesson 65

Step 6 Three columns in the spreadsheet have the title **Film**. *Access* cannot have duplicate field names so only the first one can be used.

Driving Lesson 66

Step 3 Original total £283,835.

Step 6 New total £291,835.

Driving Lesson 70

Step 1 The original prices were £4, £150, £10, £20 and £14.

Step 7 After running the query they are £4, £165, £11, £22 and £15.40.

Step 10 After modifying they are £4, £173.25, £11.55, £23.10 and £16.17.

Driving Lesson 72

Step 14 Northern Region contains the highest sales figure.

Step 15 Black.

Driving Lesson 80

Step 12 Driver's first name is Gordon.

Glossary

Bound Control	Refers to a field on a form or report that obtains its content from a specific data field on a table.
Field Properties	Define how data is entered and stored in a table.
Foreign Key	A primary key from table A, which is also used as a key field in table B is called a foreign key.
Joins	Define how relationships between tables are applied in queries.
Lookup Field	A field that can obtain (look up) its values from an existing source, either from a built in list or from another table.
Macro	An automated way of performing one or a series of actions.
One-to-many	Any one record from table A may be related to one or many records from table B.
One-to-one	One record from table A is related to one record from table B.
Parameter	A value which is used in an operation, e.g. as a query selection criteria, but can be changed each time the operation is run.
Primary Key	A field which uniquely identifies a record, e.g. telephone number in a table.
Referential Integrity	A set of rules which are applied to a relationship, to prevent or control the alteration and deletion of records in one table, that would affect records in the second table. Ensures the data in related tables is always valid.
Relationships	The ability to connect tables of data, so that no data need to be repeated.
Select Query	The basic type of query, which selects data from one or more tables.
Subdatasheet	A datasheet within a main datasheet which shows details of records from a related, subsidiary table.
Subform	A form within a main form which shows details of records from a related, subsidiary table.
Summary Calculations	In queries, these produce data calculated from a group of records without showing the individual records.
Unbound Control	Refers to a field on a form or report where the content is not from a specific data field on a table, e.g. a label.
Validation Rules	Defines the values which can be entered into a field. Entries that do not conform to the rule cannot be entered.
Wildcards	Characters which represent other unknown characters when selecting records in a query or find operation.